CONSEQUENCE BOOK SERIES ON FRESH ARCHITECTURE VOL. 3

HERAUSGEGEBEN VON / EDITED BY
iCP - INSTITUTE FOR CULTURAL POLICY

NAT CHARD

DRAWING INDETERMINATE ARCHITECTURE, INDETERMINATE DRAWINGS OF ARCHITECTURE

Springer Wien New York

iCP – Institute for Cultural Policy

Leitung / Direction:
Patrick Ehrhardt
Wolfgang Fiel

www.i-c-p.org

© 2005 Springer-Verlag/Wien
Printed in Austria
SpringerWienNewYork is a part of
Springer Science+Business Media
springeronline.com

Umschlagbilder Cover illustrations: © 2005 Nat Chard
Layout: Andreas Berlinger; London / Nat Chard; Copenhagen
Druck Printing: Holzhausen Druck & Medien GmbH
1140 Wien, Österreich

Gedruckt auf säurefreiem, chlorfrei gebleichtem Papier – TCF
Printed on acid-free and chlorine-free bleached paper
SPIN: 11404095

Mit zahlreichen (großteils farbigen) Abbildungen
With numerous (mainly coloured) illustrations

Bibliografische Informationen Der Deutschen Bibliothek
Die Deutsche Bibliothek verzeichnet diese Publikation in der
Deutschen Nationalbibliografie; detaillierte bibliografische
Daten sind im Internet über <http://dnb.ddb.de> abrufbar.

ISBN-10 3-211-25237-1 SpringerWienNewYork
ISBN-13 978-3-211-25237-6 SpringerWienNewYork

Consequence: Rendering the boundaries

´Is urban architecture in the process of becoming a technology just as outdated as extensive farming? Will architectonics become nothing more than a decadent form of dominating the earth, with consequences analogous to the unbridled exploitation of raw materials? Hasn't the decline in the number of cities also become the symbol of industrial decline and forced unemployment, the symbol of scientific materialism's failure? (...) The crisis of modernity's grand narratives, about which Lyotard speaks, betrays the presence of new technology, with the emphasis being placed, from now on, on the „means" and not on the „ends"´ (Virilio 1999).

In Anknüpfung an obiges Zitat von Paul Virilio gehen wir von der These aus, dass das Berufsbild der ArchitektIn einem grundsätzlichen poststrukturalistischen Wandel unterliegt. Mit der Immersion der digitalen Medien und elektronischen Apparate muss die Definition des architektonischen Raums einer grundsätzlichen und zeitgemäßen Revision unterzogen werden. Während das psychische Modell des modernistischen Raumparadigmas mit der Echzeiterfahrung im physischen Realraum noch kongruent war und durch die Regeln der klassischen Perspektive hinreichend beschrieben werden konnte, führt die rhizomatische Organisation der Datennetzwerke an den Schnittstellen global verteilter Userterminals zum Verlust der Wahrnehmung räumlicher Tiefe zugunsten einer kinematografischen Zeittiefe. Die Ästhetik stabiler Bilder wird durch die Ästhetik des beschleunigten Verschwindens labiler Bilder ersetzt. Räumliche Exploration erfolgt nunmehr weltumspannend an jedem beliebigen Ort, während Simultanität in elastischen Zeitintervallen erfolgt und durch die „Trägheit des Auges" bestimmt wird.

Das heisst aber auch, dass wir einen Paradigmenwechsel von der Repräsentation zur Interpretation vollziehen, der eng mit der Frage nach der Konstituierung brauchbarer Schnittstellen verbunden ist. Die von Virilio angesprochene Verlagerung von der Zielfunktion (ends) zur Wahl der Mittel (means) im Rahmen einer prozesshaften Kultur des Ereignisses entspricht gleichzeitig einer Verschiebung von der Metaebene eines dialektischen Theoriebegriffs zur mikropolitischen Praxis improvisatorischen Handels.

Mit der Auswahl der im Rahmen der Ausstellungsreihe „consequence" präsentierten ArchitektInnen soll die gängige Praxis gegenwärtiger Architekturproduktion hinterfragt werden. Sie verkörpern auf exemplarische Weise die vielfältigen Ausdrucksformen im Zuge der skizzierten Neudefinition des Berufsbilds. Die jeweiligen Tätigkeitsfelder sind durch die systematische Entwicklung partikularer Forschungsschwerpunkte gekennzeichnet, einer Art mikropolitischer und methodischer Praxis an den Rändern der eigenen Profession sowie im transdisziplinären Crossover unterschiedlicher Disziplinen. Die Arbeitsweisen haben einen Hang zum Technologischen, sind narrativ, performativ, spekulativ-ästhetisch und verfügen über ein Problembewusstsein, das auf einer konzeptuellen Ebene verankert ist oder am spezifischen Kontext festgemacht werden kann. Mit der Auswahl soll auf eine Generation aufmerksam gemacht werden, die mit ihren Arbeiten neue diskursive Räume erschließt.

Wolfgang Fiel, Hamburg, Juni 2005

Virilio, P 1999, `The overexposed city´, in Druckrey, T. & Ars Electronica (eds.), Facing The Future, MIT Press, Cambridge, pp. 276-283.

Consequence: Rendering the boundaries

`Is urban architecture in the process of becoming a technology just as outdated as extensive farming? Will architectonics become nothing more than a decadent form of dominating the earth, with consequences analogous to the unbridled exploitation of raw materials? Hasn't the decline in the number of cities also become the symbol of industrial decline and forced unemployment, the symbol of scientific materialism's failure? (...) The crisis of modernity's grand narratives, about which Lyotard speaks, betrays the presence of new technology, with the emphasis being placed, from now on, on the „means" and not on the „ends"´ (Virilio 1999).

Following up to the statement from Paul Virilio, the claim is set out, that the profession of the architect currently undergoes a significant post-structuralist change. With the immersion of digital media and electronic apparatus the definition of physical space and its perception has to be fundamentally revised. Whilst the psychological imprint of the modernistic dimension of space was specified by significant „time distances" in relation to physical obstacles, represented by the rules of perspective, the rhizomatic nature of electronic networks - accessable via the interfaces of globally distributed userterminals – has subsequently led to the loss of spatial depth in exchange for the cinematic depth of time. The believe in the enduring objectives of dualistic determinism has been succeeded by an aesthetic of the accelerated disappearance of transient images. The exhaustion of temporal distance creates a telescoping of any localization, at any position and any time, for it simultaneity is measured in elastic time-intervalls equivalent to the retinal persistance - the after image.

Likewise we face a paradigmatic change from the era of representation to one of interpretation which is closely bound to the need of creating operable interfaces. In the light of the turn from the „ends" to the „means" as aforementioned, a process-oriented culture of events would cause an improvisational turn from the meta-level of the dialectic theory-notion toward a micropolitical practice.

With the choice of architects within the scope of „consequence", well established modernistic modes of architectural representation are challenged. All of these architects embody a wide range of formal expression, as a result of their unique endeavour in research and architectonic practice alike. Their particular fields of activity are characterized by a tentative policy in exploring and augmenting the boundaries of the profession as well as to foster a prolific interchange with other disciplines. The modes of operation are technological, often do follow narratives, are performative, speculative in their account for novel aesthetics and demonstrate a sensible awareness for current local phenomena and global developments, which can be tied to a specific context or are expressed on a conceptual level. With the choice for fresh accounts from a new generation of experimental architects, we aim to launch new territorries of discourse.

Wolfgang Fiel, Hamburg, June 2005

Virilio, P. 1999, `The overexposed city´, in Druckrey, T. & Ars Electronica (eds.), Facing The Future, MIT Press, Cambridge, pp. 276-283.

Über / About iCP

Das `Institute for Cultural Policy´, wurde 2004 als unabhängige und interdisziplinäre Forschungseinrichtung in Hamburg/Deutschland gegründet. Das iCP bietet die Infrastruktur und ist diskursive Plattform für die Förderung und Weiterentwicklung des Austausches zwischen Architektur, Kunst, Wissenschaft und Industrie.

The `Institute for Cultural Policy´, was founded in 2004 as an independent and cross-disciplinary research institution in Hamburg/Germany. The iCP provides the infrastructure and is a platform for discourse fostering a prolific exchange between architecture, art, science and industry.

Danksagung / Acknowledgements

Die Herausgeber bedanken sich bei allen, die am Zustandekommen des Projekts beteiligt waren, im Speziellen Alexandra Berlinger, Andreas Berlinger, Amelie Graalfs, David Marold und Nat Chard für die ausgezeichnete Zusammenarbeit.

Acknowledgements

Nat Chard would like to thank: Karen Gamborg Knudsen and Frederik Petersen for designing the book and meticulously preparing the images. Rosie Chard for her patient and careful proof reading. Eva Ravnborg, Gudrun Krabbe, Maya Lahmy, Morten Petersen, Christina Back, Karin Bech, Nadin Heinrich and Amanda Taarup Betz for help in preparing the accompanying exhibition. For supporting his work through publications: Neil Spiller, Jonathan Hill, Peter Cook, Bob Sheil, Nick Callicott, Chris Thurlbourne, C.J.Lim and Marc Armengaud. Michael Anderson for his generous and complete transparency with his research material on J.P.Wilson. For indulgent and helpful conversations about the work: Florian Koehl, Mette Thomsen, Mark Ruthven, Peter Cook, Michael Anderson, Simon Ingvartesen and on a few but highly valued occasions, Mike Webb. And for the invitation to be part of the iCP project, Wolfgang Fiel.

All photographs by the author except where noted.

Pairs of similar images are stereoscopic and can be resolved into a 3D view by using stereo lorgnettes (available from Agar Scientific: sales@agar.co.uk)

Table of contents:

Introduction by Peter Cook

Most of the time we are hearing about 'surface'. If not, we're hearing about process, we're hearing about the mathematics of the inevitable rolling-out of digitalised response patterns. Some of the results look lovely. Some look boring. Few have any sensitivity. Few are able to 'chatter'. Yet they have become the tidal wave of architecture, ready to engulf the mainstream scene and leave it in a state as never before.

Yet lurking in a quiet corner of Europe and about to bounce over into a quiet corner of North America there is an architectural intellect of real originality and real power whose work has the stuff of discovery and quizzicality that offers so much more than the tidal wave.

For one thing it dwells upon a series of deep observations: it is always looking, looking and then looking again at the curious edges of a situation. Both in his observational work and in his designed juxtapositions there comes a point where the very 'quaintness' of a scene becomes too tantalising for Nat Chard to leave alone.

At first, it seems as if he is a quiet chap, in the great tradition of English collectors, English explorers. English boffins, English narrative artists: all of whom have an ability to assemble-together a series of pieces or episodes that seem very unlikely as elements of a coherent piece, but, as they are quietly explained, as they take a grip on us, they begin to weave a spell.

Years ago, Nat delved into the stomach. The resulting airbrushed drawings were at once shocking and evocative. They said much about language, about space and thus, about architecture. They drew our attention towards the body - almost as a piece of urbanism. Only the late John Hejduk and Michael Webb seem to match it. They too construct bodies and intestinal insertions: in Hejduk's case couched within a spiritual framework that pervaded his manner, his anecdotes and the whole of his Cooper Union School. In Webb's case, the propositions sit upon each other's shoulders as a series of technological pirouettes, Chard's process is more crab-like.

He collects naturalistic panoramas that were produced in museums and then moves in on them as concentrations of the real and the unreal, the true and the distorted. He becomes obsessed by three-dimensionality and viewpoint.

Yet as a designer, he produces machines that will observe, look, photograph, draw, compare: all of which become much more interesting and telling than the conditions or objects that are being observed, etc. He starts to use computer-cutting techniques and he casts moulds. The cut objects and the moulds far outshine the phenomena that they try to legitimise. Whilst still living in London, he designed a stunning set of extension-artefacts that would have converted his dreary grey villa into something akin to a mixture of the Golden Pavilion in Kyoto and the lollipop palaces that you see in shops that sell seaside rock.

This is an English characteristic, this ability to allow a tatty, mundane or matter-of-fact condition to be the springboard for something imaginative and wonderful, without cheekiness or the blink of an eyelid.

His work as a teacher has of course been a mirror of this imagination, Nat has led his troops towards the world of investigatory machines, with eyes, wings, legs, cameras, lenses, tabulations, trajectories, scatter-patterns, cones of vision. Usually they have been highly aesthetic and quite romantic. Of course, Nat would sternly deny such Romanticism and then, when he thinks that you're not looking, he will give a knowing little smile.

For an ostensibly quiet person, he is an astute judge of character and of people's interplay. This is why he is a member of that very small band of people who can design with a multiplicity of content-types. Amongst his contemporaries are a number of people who can do this kind of thing if they set up a 'séance' - usually quasi-historicist or 'antique' around it. Somehow though, I feel that his work is entirely 'modern': in that it seeks not just to verify a theorem or the efficacy of an atmosphere or an aura: more to discover what might be out there.

The Nat Chard space explorer will, like that of Mike Webb, find something quite weird and unexpected out there. Webb may be unwilling to let the rocket out of his hand, Chard will probably have erected such an extraordinary launch platform (culled from the serendipity of an agile eye) that it far outshines any likely nearby planet. Somewhat extraordinarily, he holds all the ingredients of a spatial architecture: that can see round corners, grasp volume, track edges and paths, scratch life out of dead material.
He understands much.

ticularly the relationships between Malmö and Copenhagen at night. Collaborating with him underlined two keys aspects of his thought and practice, also engaged in Troll :

- the subversion of the city's program described as a body matrix, throughout sub-programs diverting what seemed to be pre-set for good
- the design of drawing tools that would re-project the drawer's experience as an interpretative and potentially operative dimension of the drawing for the viewer

Troll ? Conducted by AWP -a Paris based inter-disciplinary collective, this program regards the night time as a new (last ?) frontier for urban prospective. Envisioning cities in their duration rather than in their spatial extension/volumes leads to the observation of the existence of several cities wired into or onto one abstract main structure whose meaning becomes questionable. Confronted with global complexity and contradictions, the night time enables us to restart a question such as: what can we design from?

Fast accessibility and flexibility at night are two characteristics that feed a focus on the metropolitan scale: it is only then that one can experience issues that usually appear in Dutch architecture prospective pamphlets. Transporting our body at the scale of the metropolis suddenly changes the mental map of who is entitled to discuss the scale issues.

Mobility is the tool to read, map and operate the urban night as a furtive landscape, a body experience of transit and uncertain perceptions. Mobility is the factor that keeps a temporal reading of the city alive (following Bergson's distinction between instant based time which somehow equals space and pure duration that needs a perceptive intuition to be understood).

Mobility is also the context for street intervention tactics on the metropolitan scale that ad-

Troll Roma on the tangenziale.

Night time mobility by Marc Armengaud [5]

Questions raised while collaborating with Nat Chard within the Troll Protocol research and experiment program on night time mobility.

I tried to reach Nat Chard's interest for urban indeterminate conditions in favour of the Troll Protocol that has been developed since 2003 in Europe and North America, and started with a study of the Øresund mobility circle and par-

dress to non-specialized audiences. Furtive cat-walks and ephemeral mousetraps…

For instance, developing a temporary bus line, hi-jacked live from a public radio that was broadcasted in the busses, taking over the drivers' directions to take Romans from the Capitoline Hill towards far away peripheries: the Tangenziale -a suspended motorway, became a pedestrian path looking at modern ruins, the 1Km long social housing unit Corviale became the site of a collaborative light constellation, and the Pinetta Sachetti hosted virtual gardens that one could navigate, guided by sounds. This Troll Passeggiata (April 2004), designed by AWP with Nat Chard, aimed at reverting the main pattern that drives hundred of thousands of roman to the very centre of the city every Saturday night. As a result, Troll aims at leaving traces behind: amongst the inhabitants, the elects, the institutions and associations, the creatives and the researchers that participate in the making of these researches and experiments. Traces could be the suspension of the decision to destroy the Tangenziale, or creating a habit to use the hill behind Corviale as a public space at night.

The Troll Protocol reveals another urban geography, built from human links rather than needs, of temporary dimensions and rough conflicts whose importance only comes to the daytime as a vague rumour. Even though the few facts we know are striking: up to 3 millions persons may travel through the Paris metropolitan area (+/-12 M) on a week night: where to? How? Why? With whom?

Researching this field means starting from nothing, since very little data is accessible or even exists. Observation and experimentation often seem stronger tools to set contemporary questions. If we miss academic references, we can nevertheless identify the context: growing pressures from international firms to develop 24/7 market shares, and symmetric exploitation of the fear of darkness by local politicians, are suddenly incorporated in the wider context of city branding fierce competition. Under the ruthless inspiration of sociologists/consultants like Richard Florida , main European and American cities scheme the redevelopment of their nightlife as to enter the « superliga of the appetizing cities ». Every city should try to develop its' night time specificities in order to be internationally desirable, and attract tourists, but moreover, corporate employees that will care to live in the city centre (and pay taxes) and consume leisure and culture intensely. This cocktail would be able to attract companies, who try to employ high achievers. The conclusion of this position appears to be that only people with certain marketing profiles optimise city life. An example would be the gay community since gays are, in marketing terms, perceived to be night time people and are seen to be one of the leading consumer groups. This position tries to cynically hi-jack communities subject to marketing taxonomies such as the gay liberation movement, framing night's development through the hyper-determined lens of community marketing.

We are indeed very far from urban indeterminacy! Gender marketing has influenced urban identity design to a point were crude cynicism becomes the flag for tolerance and cultural innovation. Night time is the reverse of the day… Should cities remain indeterminate or should they become specific based, and ground their development on its preferable communities? Of course R. Florida's concepts are generated from a strictly US context, but he is nevertheless exporting them worldwide. Communitizing the night time, in order to extend profit and taxes in the city centres… This is also reminding us that our interest for mobility is not only for the transport logistic, but a social understanding of democracy: the ability to forge your own destiny translated into mobility patterns in the social scale, the gender rates, the geographical migrations. In that context, public transportation is maybe the last non-commercial generator of non-segregated public spaces .

If our collaboration with Nat Chard was so interesting, it is because he raised the question of the necessity of an indeterminate architecture and city conception. Not only to enable formal innovation and radical creation, but because the key meanings of what architecture is meant for, are in question.
The functional metaphysic of architecture sees the program of the city directly answering body functions: providing conditions for eating, sheltering, transporting, heating, working, What if the body's

functions acquire autonomous functions? First as to sophisticate the body logic to a point were biology is no more the reference point, but development and progress its own matrix. Doubles within the simple. The urban body goes other ways, through its original canvas, reorganizing priorities and information systems. Then we are encouraged to look at the city as a cyborg (or actually a whole family of them), keeping its artificial extensions secret because they might alter the hierarchy of rational functions. Nat's work is both confronting itself to the body logic (including its negation through sub-systems) and pointing at the consequences that architecture should take up from this dynamic or dialectic. Prospective is not a subversion of the imaginary against reality; it is a moral and political necessity. What can we design from? Ask the body.

The night time is primarily meant for one key body function: sleep. Architecture provides shelters for sleep, but what becomes of the rest of the city's program ? Is it also set to sleep? In that sense, the work Nat is conducting faced an expected difficulty: what his thoughts oppose to, were suddenly not confronted to any resistance. The material itself vanished (body functions). What happens then?
Of course there is a city at night (24/7 shifts) and a night life: are these parallel systems? They might refer to primary body needs (sex, transgression, excess, socializing…), but not necessarily those that architecture faces as a mission. Or is it the assignment that is not adapted?

As a negation of the daily body, or as the first artificial extension, cities at night reset the approach. This reverse angle underlines the strength of Nat Chard's interpretation: because it is at night that we can observe the strength of sub-programs that reshape completely the context and the expression of shape production:

transformation, transmutation is the essence of the body experience at night: experimenting movement/displacement to a point where identity can be left aside for a while.

Troll also looks at the night time street intervention tactics that went stronger and stronger since the 90's: free parties, night time demonstrations, street sports at night... But if these strategies/actions mostly derive from the quest for more fun (however important is the thrill of braking the code), it might be that these practices point at a reality that can be radicalized for itself: moving around at night, out the daily patterns is a key to urban understanding and reconfiguration. Both for the night and the day. And then again comes a need for representing what we experience and choose to answer to. Perception, a technical/metaphysical question of drawing? Nat contributed with its night time mobility drawing machine: since navigating at night is collecting every few visual information, but also other body information such as those measured by the feet, this map had to be a 3D one. A robot to unfold dimensions and recreate a sense of orientation. Being lost in the dark is a radical body experience that we might start from if we try to answer questions such as: can we design from the Night time indeterminacy?

Notes:
[1] And also : the Stalker collective, Per Henriksen, Erico Molteni, Michael Rudolph, Sigrund Langner, Gaetano Di Stasio, Matthieu Mevel, GianMaria Sforza, Sari Myöhänen, TAL.
[2] Cf « the Creative Class », Richard Florida.
[3] Except maybe at night, then public transport is in practice often not accessible to women, children and older persons.
[4] Alvar Aalto would for a long time refuse to have his buildings lighten, because he believed buildings also need to sleep.
[5] MA is a philosopher and artist. Member of the AWP interdisciplinary collective for architecure, landscape and design (http://trollawp.free.fr/, http://www.awp.fr/)

The hall and the staircase sequence, 1992. A space that is sensitive to the desires and anxieties of the occupant. A second figure enters via the staircase and disturbs the space created by the first person. Airbrush.

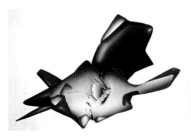

Context

The construction of the architectural program encourages an approach that sees architecture as a prediction, imagining what will take place in and around it and trying to support that action in appropriate ways. The precision of an architecture's tight fit to an imagined program might support such a program if it takes place but it will also prescribe the sort of occupation or coerce the occupants into certain forms of occupation. Users will mark the architecture with their actions during occupation, leaving traces that suggest how it should be inhabited. Between the advance prescription and this durational inscription, the architecture absorbs much of its meaning. There are many delights in this con-

gation signal
ference on the
s of a desire
itive space,
4. Normally
space detects
electronic sig-
from the body
rm itself. The
ext is supplied
elecommuni-
on and naviga-
signals that
also picked
Stereoscopic
Airbrush on
roid transfer +
nation figure.

struction, not least a structure of meaning that can be both poetic, purposeful and can locate us in broader cultural and practical worlds. It also provides a level of comfort where we know our place in such an architecture without having to engage in it, concentrating instead, perhaps, on the content it supports. The work discussed in this book recognizes the lure of such benefits but asks the question as to whether we want to be so passive and as a consequence, how is it possible for architecture to also take its meaning from now? A further question is do we want the architecture to be so passive, slumped in the comfort of complacent understandings and, as a consequence, should its role also be to provoke as well as support? Of course there are times when the undemanding comfort of program-matic conformity is a relief but also times when

it is claustrophobic. Or to put it another way, if we want to be active or implicated in the world, how might architecture support that condition?

I am not making a manifesto for the indeterminate condition. My study is to ask how such a condition is possible. But to start with I would like to clarify what such a position is about. In an essay about the relationship between determinism and the sublime Jean-Francois Lyotard cites a short unfinished text by Barnett Newman stating that his paintings were not concerned with a manipulation of

Feedback pe
tions in desi
sensitive spa
1993. Airbru:
Polaroid trar

space or image but with a sensa- tion of time. He adds that he does not mean the kind of time laden by nostalgia, drama or references to history. Lyotard writes, "Newman surely cannot have been thinking of the 'present instant,' the one that tries so hard to claim territory between the future and the past, but manages only to be devoured by them. That 'now' is one of the temporal 'extasies' that have been analyzed from Augustine's day all the way to Edmund Husserl, ac- cording to a line of thought that has attempted to compose time out of consciousness. Newman's now is a stranger to consciousness and cannot be composed in terms of it. Rather, it is what dismantles consciousness, what dis- misses consciousness; it is what consciousness cannot formulate, and even what conscious- ness forgets in order to compose itself". After explaining how disciplines and schools set up determining systems he continues "All intellec- tual disciplines and institutions take for granted that not everything has been said, written, or re- corded, that words already heard or pronounced are not the last words. 'After' a sentence, 'after' a colour, comes another sentence, another col- our. One doesn't necessarily know which, but it is possible to guess if credence is given to the rules that chain one sentence to another, cue one colour to another-rules preserved in pre- cisely the institutions of the past and future that I mention above. The school, the program, the

Durational feedback drawing for desire sensitive space for two people, 1993. Study of relationship between personal projection of space, recollection of the previous condition, context and the feedback loop. Airbrush and acrylic.

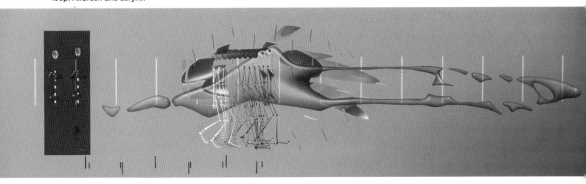

project-all proclaim that after such a sentence, such another sentence or at least such sort of a sentence is mandatory, that one kind of sentence is mandatory, that one kind of sentence is permitted, while another is forbidden". He goes on to say that these schools "forget the possibility that nothing will happen, that words, colours, forms, or sounds will be absent, that some sentence will be the last, that one day the bread will not arrive. This is the misery that the painter encounters with plastic surface, or the musician with an acoustic surface; it is the misery the thinker sees in the desert of thought. It isn't simply a matter of the empty canvas or the empty page, at the 'beginning' of a work, but of each instance of something being imminent, which makes a question of every question mark, every "and now what?" We tend to assume that noth-

ing will happen without the feeling of anxiety, a term much elaborated on by modern philosophers of existence and the unconscious. This gives anticipation, if we really mean anticipation, a predominantly negative value. In fact suspense can also be accompanied by pleasure-for instance, pleasure of the unknown-and even by joy-the joy, to paraphrase Baruch Spinoza, the intensification of being, that the event induces. This probably brings up contradictory feelings. It is at the very least a sign of the question mark itself. The question can adapt itself to any tone, as Jaques Derrida would

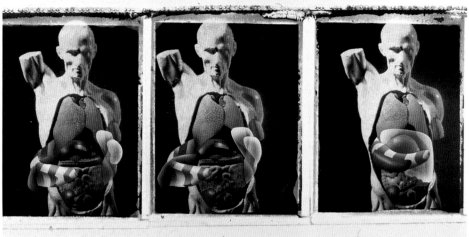

Early body
project to ta
possession o
the city usin
agined bio- a
nanotechnol
gies (see bo
projects), 19
Two drawing
left (shown v
the synthetic
gans opened
for illustratio
make up ste
pair. Airbrus
Polaroid tran

say. But the mark of the question is the "now", now in the sense that nothing might happen".

While this refers to artistic production it can also be seen as a metaphor for our broader engagement with the world. The projects I describe in the first chapter relate to this. The architectural program prescribes occupation in many ways and makes audacious claims about how it might support our bodies in the city. My body projects question these relationships by altering the specific performances of the body that touch these programs. By erasing the

prescription of the program (if architecture is as precise in its programmatic relationship with the body as it claims) my projects ask how we might open up the meaning of the city again and each of us be able to take possession of it in our own way. These studies emerged out of a series of projects that are documented in this introduction.

The consistent question in this work relates to the moment of authorship in architecture, looking at how that might take place during occupation rather than in advance. By trying to make architecture that responded to our desires and anxieties as well as provoking us and at the same time working out the social implications of such a construction it was clear that I needed a greater understanding of our perceptual an

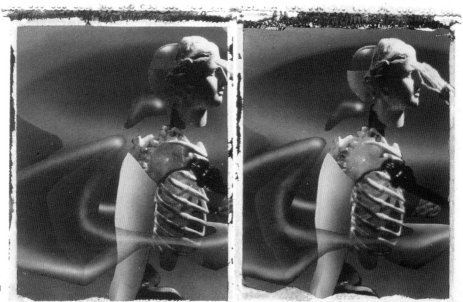

...eriencing the ...ire sensitive ...ce, 1994. Air- ...sh on Polaroid ...sfer.

social faculties. For the architecture to operate successfully, its systems would need a level of prescription in their behaviour that could be seen as equivalent to the programmatic prescription in a more passive architecture. The body projects are in part a consequence of this problem, but also very practically of the technology that I was looking at to achieve my ends. The micro technologies that would make such an architecture possible seemed more appropriate inside the body than out.

A small apartment project develops the question of programmatic indeterminacy, largely by fragmenting familiar programs and allowing those fragments to be reassembled as if words in a surrealist game.

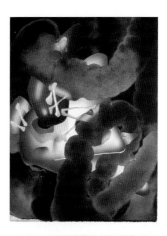

Detail, early body project, 1992. Airbrush on Polaroid transfer.

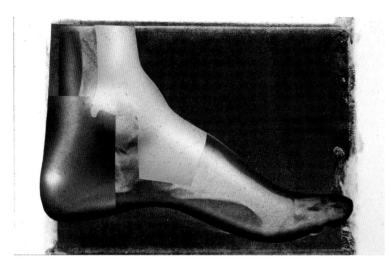

Perception
drawings of foot,
to be read with
drawings op-
posite, 1994.

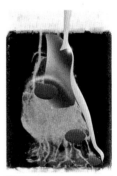

Perception draw-
ings for desire
sensitive space,
1993.Airbrush on
Polaroid transfer.

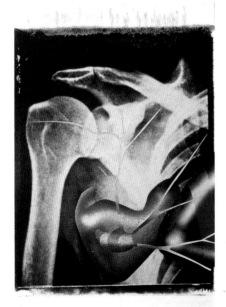

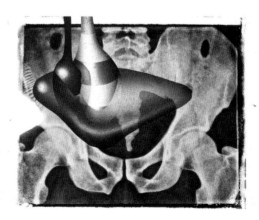

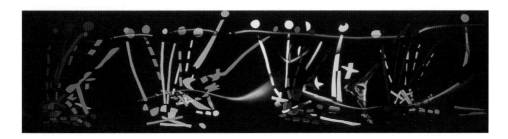

Out of all this work, there is a troubling question that refuses to go away. Even when you make an architecture that takes its meaning from its occupation, it still has to be proposed as a thing in advance of that occupation and for that to happen it has to be designed. To design such an architecture I need the same relationship to what I draw as the occupant has with the architecture. To draw indeterminate architecture I need to make indeterminate drawings of architecture. This asks the question of how drawings become architecture and the relationship the author or the interested observer has with the drawing. Or how is the drawing able to support the condition of "now" analysed by Lyotard? My strategy has been to look at our spatial relationship with the drawing, or how we become implicated in a drawing through our position relative to the picture plane.

Top: Durational scan of two figures walking and the consequential space, 1994. Airbrush.

Lower: Durational study of space between lower legs of two people walking.1994, Acrylic.

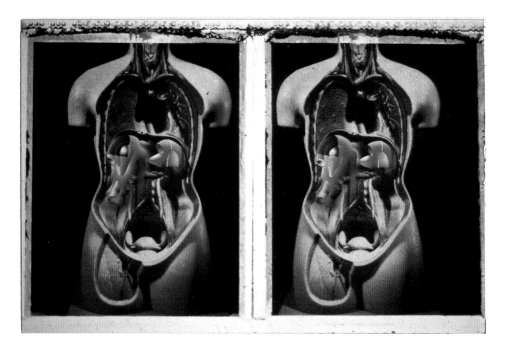

House, layer 1, 1996. Second generation body project where almost all the new organs attempt to use contemporary technology. The new implants work in a feedback loop with the natural organs. They reproduce the programmatic performance claimed by the traditional house. The sequence of layers show the build up of implants, this layer showing the main circulatory and respiratory pumps. Stereoscopic pair. Airbrush on Polaroid transfer.

Body projects

My two principle criticisms of the active architecture that follows our desires and anxieties (the work documented in the introduction) were that too much was asked of the architecture and that I was not using the technology in an appropriate way. If, in an indeterminate system, the architecture's behaviour tries to do too much it starts to deny us the sort of engagement that implicates us in the space. By interpreting us so thoroughly the opportunity for ambiguity is lost. The miniaturisation of technology in the materials and processes I was using seemed clumsy and missing its opportunity in making large building components. Both issues are addressed in a series of projects where the architecture is built inside rather than outside the body. The archi-

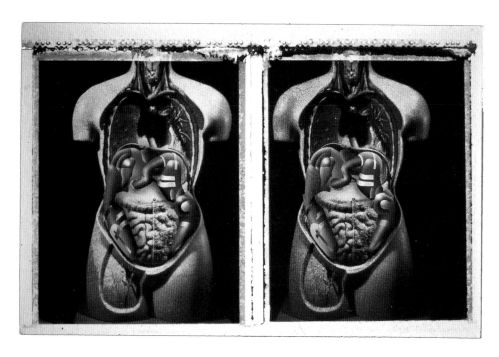

...use, layer
...996. Filters
... second-
...pumps.
...reoscopic
... Airbrush
...Polaroid
...sfer.

tecture inhabits us. In fact, I dropped the new technologies after the early body projects as on the one hand they allowed me complete freedom to do anything as, at least at the time; they were as much projections of scientist's imaginations as material realities and so offered no critical resistance. On the other hand I did not have the medical knowledge to understand the full implication of these technologies and therefore could not push them to a conceptual limit. So I will concentrate on the question of how these projects discuss our role in architecture and the city.

The second generation of this project was intensely practical. Reacting to the lack of resistance in the first generation in the first attempt I calculated flow rates for blood, air, food and fluids. The system duplicated the existing organs that are most closely associated with the most programmatic sites relating architecture to the body. This synthetic system was connected to the original system in a series of feedback loops. The apparatus and its installation is discussed in eight pairs of stereoscopic drawings showing each layer relating to its surrounding natural organs. Six more drawings (see House X-rays) discuss the social implications of the apparatus. It constructs a largely invisible architecture whose consequence is as much to do with how the architecture is

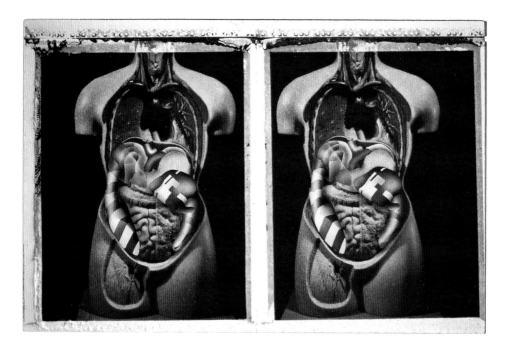

House, layer 3, 1996. Digestive power converter and storage. Stereoscopic pair. Airbrush on Polaroid transfer.

programmed as with its capability. They show a person wearing the architecture in a position to take an accompanying X-ray. The normal photograph reveals bulges, a formal transparency that reveals the new organs inside while the X-rays are also selective about what they give away. As with the experience of wearing this architecture, ideas are only partially given away.

The third generation was made due to real technology overtaking what I had drawn' as well as the need to edit the equipment down to what might really be needed to

have an urban consequence. The architecture is a system that allows several options of equipment and almost infinite settings. The conceptual possibilities of the work are outlined in the following essay that I wrote for a book celebrating the career of the exceptional urbanist Professor Luise King .

Redesigning the city inside the body.

After a few busy days working, she has some time to herself in the city before her flight home early the next morning. She has been here several times before, sometimes alone or with a friend and sometimes with students. There are a few new places but mostly she visits old haunts, especially the complex and hidden intertwined courtyards. One route from a grand

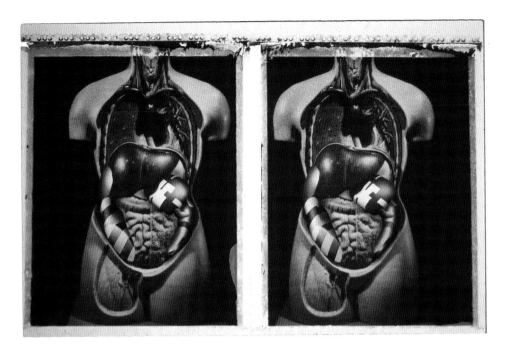

se, layer
996. Organ
page
agement.
eoscopic
Airbrush
Polaroid
sfer.

old tearoom is locked today, but it is possible to see the destination and catch up with it by going back into the street and sliding into another discrete opening. This one is very elaborate, but some of the others have been simpler, though no more ordered. This morning she stopped for cake in a favourite café and now she is looking back into the tea room, where a minute ago she had tried to find a way through to her present position, and she realises she has been walking for most of the day yet feels neither hunger nor thirst. Although familiar, the places she has visited are also strange and alive again for her, not quite as fresh as the first visit but pleasingly different. Not that she has remembered them wrongly or that they have changed much. More that she has changed. The city is as it has ever been and the way it is curated (for in many ways

it is as much a museum as any of the other explanations of this city) it is as it ever will be. But for her it is different and the thrill of this difference leads her to speculate how she might want it next time and reminisce about those long drifts she had optimistically made as a student hoping for the city to give her back as much as she projected into it. Then it was pleasant but frustrating. The company had been good and the walks long and revealing but the city had rarely been able to reciprocate her indulgence.

Thinking back to the rich choco-

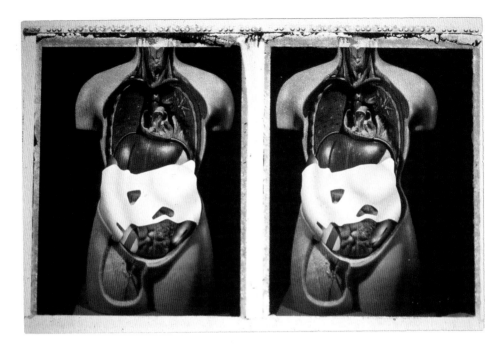

House,
Layer 5, 1996.
Heat shield.
Stereoscopic
pair. Airbrush
on Polaroid
transfer.

late and coffee cake of that morning, she realises she had gone there to see the place and eat the cake as another reminiscence. The last time she had been there the slices had been too small for her hunger but too rich to order a second slice. That last visit was punctuated by several deviations to recommended cafés and a small restaurant that they had come across in the way one dreams one will in a foreign city but rarely finds. This punctuation had coloured the city with subplots and distractions that had made the courtyards much more isolated, or at least episodic,

than today, where they have been a continuous weave in and out of the more familiar fabric of the city. Her scepticism about the architecture that inhabits her subsides. All along she has understood the possibility of such an architecture. Instinctively she was fascinated by the first generation but after reading about it had thought it conceptually much too generic and practically too bulky for her slender frame. But the second generation is much more compact and tuneable and the proliferation of aftermarket suppliers had made it possible for her to specify exactly the range of conditions she wished the city to provide. The latest version is also much easier to install, with only a local anaesthetic for someone as fit as her.

In the three weeks since she has occupied, or

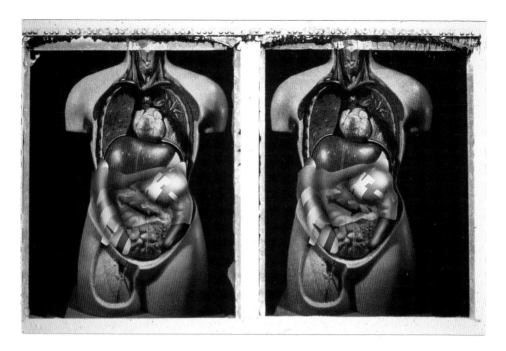

se, layer 6,
. Central
rol unit.
roscopic
Airbrush
olaroid
fer.

more accurately perhaps, been occupied by such an architecture she has experienced a number of side effects, not all of them displeasing. As the evening gets colder she can stay out longer without a coat, but there is a moment when a strange frisson rushes through her body when the new synthetic organs of her internal architecture work hard to produce enough heat while her extremities feel the evening chill. It sometimes works the other way when it is hot and sunny and she can feel the implants cooling inside her, making her interior feel continuous with the outside world. She has always been a strong walker but now she is unstoppable. She has felt these things today and as she walks into the shadows of yet another courtyard that spirals in on itself behind a church she momentarily catches that funny feeling again. It feels para-

doxical to her that this internal architecture has given her so much autonomy that she can experience the old city with some detachment, something that has lost its given meanings and is available again for her, not just through interpretation but in a phenomenal way. Perhaps similar to her new experience of the cake she had earlier tried to use as an agent of recollection but had discovered that her relationship to it had shifted profoundly. She wonders how long this will last. Will it be like the 3D film she saw the other week where the effect wore off after ten minutes and the director had to

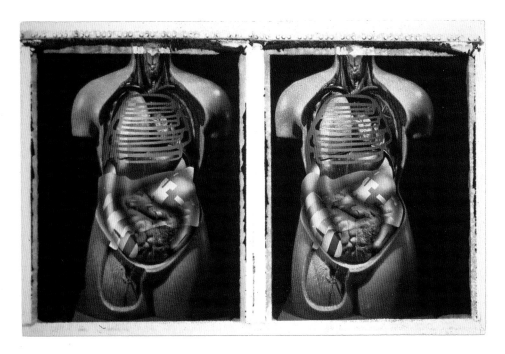

House, layer 7, 1996. Heat exchanger. Stereoscopic pair. Airbrush on Polaroid transfer.

play all manner of tricks to keep the audience alert to the spectacle. It is time to find out. In her hotel room last night after the group she was working with had returned from their evening meal she had read more of the manual and had anticipated today by preparing a number of presets. The surgeon (architect) who had installed the implant had advised her to keep it on the default setting for the first three weeks so her body could accept the synthetic organs in a stable condition. During her checkup last week everything was fine and she had been encouraged to try out new settings within the in-

termediate performance band. During the meal she had drunk quite a lot, but the implant had filtered the effect and she had spent much of the night wondering how to change the city. She also wondered about this loss of sleep and how to use this time, as she has yet to see the full potential of her new alertness at night. While her body now needs much less rest, she wonders if the time she spends dreaming is quite enough.

The manual explains the most obvious relationships between the body and architecture and the city. By way of introduction it suggests a few adjustments to the default setting that will have predictable effects on the city but carefully explains " If architecture or the city's programmatic claims are true, if they can support the practical and cultural performance of the

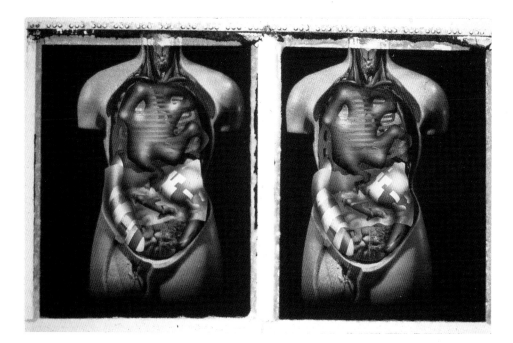

se, layer
96. Res-
ory vessel
works in
nstant
ne
onship
natural
s so that
ne system
thes in
ther
thes out.
eoscopic
Airbrush
olaroid
fer.

body as tightly as they claim, then by changing the performance of the body you necessarily change the city". Of course the apparatus had many of the performative aspects of architecture, so could to a large extent replace buildings and she had wondered about the implications of this on the city if much of the population took to this internal architecture. But it was the aspect that she had just re-read that had attracted her most to such an architecture. Having spent her working life trying to understand the inner depths of the city she had worried that on retirement she might fall out of love with it. By installing the implants she could open up the whole question again. It was not so much specific adjustments to the city that she longed for, much more the hope that it would remain ever new for her. She understands the practical aspect of the architecture that she now weares. That it concentrates on those performances of the body that architecture claims to support in a prosthetic way such as hygiene, heating and cooling, almost everything to do with eating and digestion, some aspects of rest, etc. But today she was ready to try out other critical aspects that she had imagined less convincing. She had made her presets to ask questions of privacy. There is one obvious aspect that the manual points out " Remember, the way you change the city with your internal architecture is just for you, you do not change it for anybody else". But

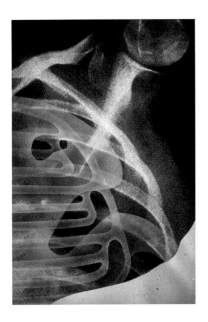

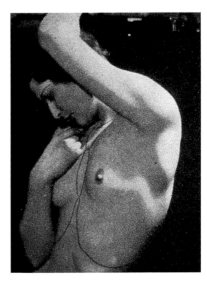

House, X-ray with partial revelation of heat exchanger and respiratory implants and positioning photograph for that view, 1996. Note the implant revealed by pushing into her skin just below the ribcage. Airbrush on inkjet print.

she wanted more than that, something she had always wanted from the city and even without the apparatus had sometimes found, but not as often as she would like. She wanted to be with the city but also alone.

The surgeon had advised slow transitions to start with, preferably while resting so the body could learn to cope with the adjustments. She stopped at a restaurant – they would close soon and there was nothing her architecture could do about that. She did all the things that her apparatus had postponed for her and chose a simple meal. As the room is warm and her apparatus is still learning about the speed with which her body adapts to temperature changes she experiences another of those funny feelings as the natural and synthetic systems find their equilibrium. A little uncertain whether this is really a pleasure, she wonders if she will become desensitized to these occurrences. As the food arrives she knows she has already stored enough energy to take her through tomorrow, but wants the meal to reconnect into the time structure of the city. She has had to eat more than usual since acquiring her new architecture, for it also requires feeding. Her choices from the menu now have nothing to do with hunger or virtue or responsibility to her constitution. Food has to satisfy her in other more sensual ways and she has already developed greater sensitiv-

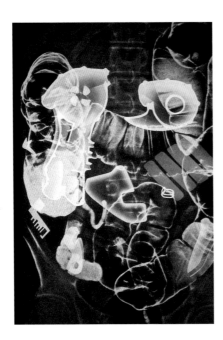

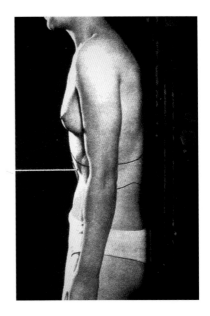

ities to these pleasures, detecting the regional origin of certain vegetables, for instance. One of the things that has annoyed her during the last three weeks is the lack of tiredness or hunger or thirst. She had been warned, and has studiously drunk more water than she would usually. Her body will adapt but at the moment she feels a little like one of those Californian lawns that glows healthily year round, rain or drought, on account of the irrigation system and plentiful sun. Her preset has taken hold and she can feel slight differences that she tries to relate to her intentions when she set them last night. But she is not yet sure about this new relationship with food. While the apparatus takes away the risk of gaining weight if she over indulges, this has never been a problem for her and this loss of edge has not blunted her desire for fine tasting food.

The new setting is pure speculation. Working beyond the most obvious programmatic performance, she is using abnormal settings for the time of year in a hope of making a private condition. While walking through the city she feels conspicuously underdressed for the conditions, yet hardly feels the cold. The weather is not too bad and she does not stand out any more than those too proud to wear appropriate clothing on the way to their night out. It is hard to tell if the privacy she hopes for exists, indeed, it feels a little like it

Layer 1

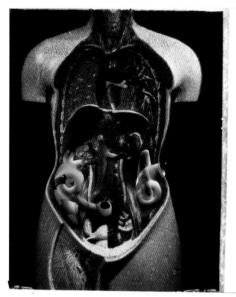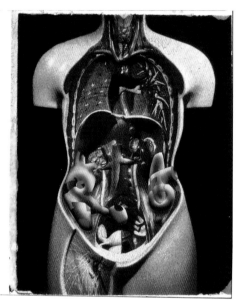

did when she went on those drifts hoping for so much and not sure how much she got back. But then she notices a couple walking towards her. He is well covered up but she is wearing low cut jeans and a t-shirt that leaves a gap to her belt about the width of a hand. The oblique light from the street lamp casts enough shadow to reveal two small bulges, recognizable to aficionados as the consequence of the fluid and air pumps and filters of a first generation internal architecture. She doesn't think the girl has seen her looking, but as they pass the girl says to her "what is your city like tonight"?

Above and next page: Third generation body project including images overleaf, 2002. The narrative text refers to this version of the project. It is revised to take account of advances in medical technology since House, for instance through miniaturization. Unlike House the implants do not constitute a doubling of all existing organs, instead being much more selective and tuned for particular spatial consequences. Otherwise it is conceptually similar to House. The layers are all stereoscopic pairs and are airbrush on Polaroid transfers, while the X-rays are airbrush on Inkjet.

Below: Folded maps. Understanding the revised body's new relationship to the city.

Layer 2

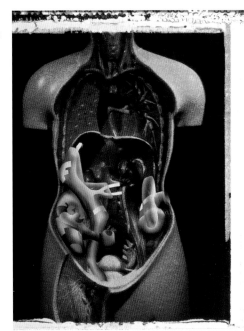
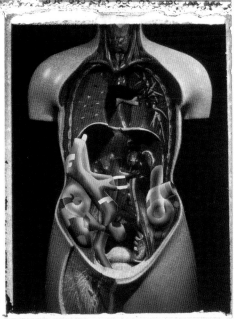

Layer 3

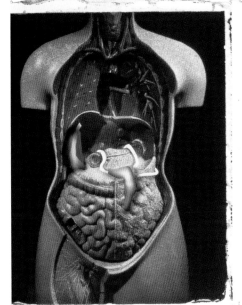
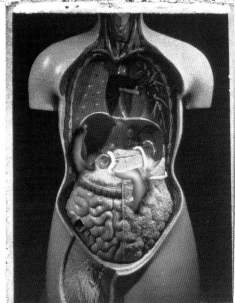

Layer 4

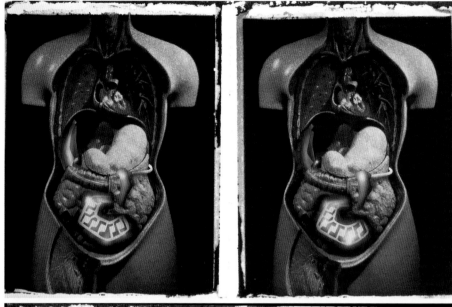

Layer 5

Layer 6

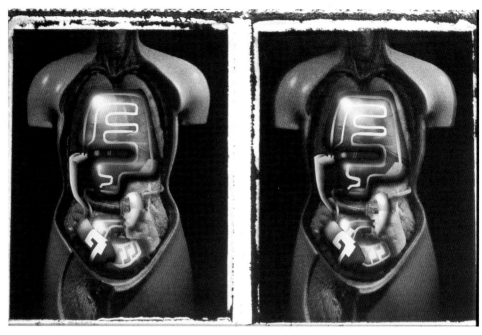

X-rays.
Airbrush
on inkjet
prints.

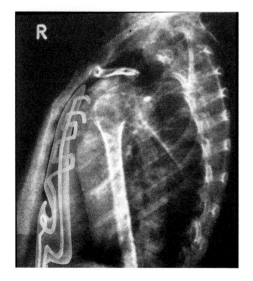

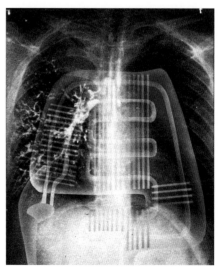

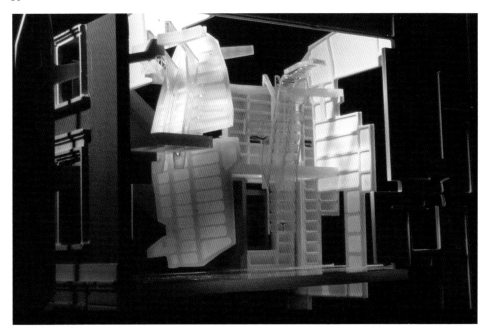

House

A proposal to extend an apartment in Camden, North London, that occupied the top two floors of a late nineteenth century semi detached house. The existing front elevation is retained (a planning requirement) but the rest of the existing apartment is demolished and replaced by a steel structure that goes down to the ground. As well as supporting the apartment the steel frame is used as the defining fixed spatial element. The existing brick structure was not strong enough to support the intended dynamic loads and the

new structure allowed the apartment to expand beyond the confinement of those walls.

The project asks questions about how something as permanent as a house, something that is used continuously by the same people, can retain an open content. As with the body projects the house flirts with the possibility of subverting programs while not concentrating on programmatic indeterminacy – it is always intended as a house, for instance. A tactic in this house is to fragment elements that are typical programs, say kitchen, bathroom, workshop, library, bedroom etc. and set them up so parts of each program can be endlessly recombined with others. The behaviour or programming of the assembly of elements would be a mixture of intention, under the control of the inhabitants, and provocations

Left: View
through party
wall into main
space showing
picture planes
and steel
structure be-
hind retained
front elevation.

Below: View from side
elevation, 1999. The fixed
programmatic fragments
are from the left, the
library shelves, the staircase and the wet compo-
nents of the bathroom (top
floor) and kitchen (lower
floor) next to the existing
front elevation.

Right: Three
quarters view
from garden
looking at the
same elements
as previous
image, 1999.

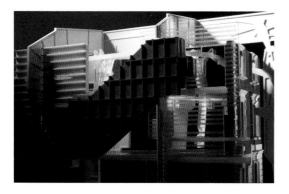

where the house would rearrange itself while everyone is out. The harder to move fragments such as staircase and wet bathroom and kitchen fittings are fixed on the periphery of the house and make up the outside wall. The more mobile pieces are on tracks that run along the inside edge of the top floor gallery. They are mounted to the back of large screens that face into the two story main space. The screens are used to make a large picture plane that gets composited with views through the fragments to the outside world. They move with their attached program-matic elements. These pieces also make up the balustrade or wall to the inside of the gallery.

There are many permutations of elements rang-ing from practical assemblies like a mixture of kitchen and workshop pieces, or bedroom and bathroom for example. But there are also seemingly stranger com-binations such as workshop and bedroom or library and kitchen. As the inhabitants become more used to these sorts of provoca-tions the sense of absurd might dissolve and be replaced by small moments of realization and pleas-ure or the sort of irritation that would incite conscious adjust-ments. Beyond the combinations the position of familiar pieces – my bed, my clothes, for instance, or the common services would pro-voke the inhabitants to continually rediscover the dwelling and some-times become infuriated with it.

32

Right: **Study for further development of wet services on external wall, 1999. Stereoscopic pair. Airbrush on Polaroid transfer.**

Right: **Study for internal programmatic fragments, 1999. Stereoscopic pair. Airbrush on Polaroid transfer.**

Above: **Study for a non-programmatic external fragment, 1999. Stereoscopic pair. Airbrush on Polaroid transfer.**

Left: **Alternative study to the image above, 1999. Stereoscopic pair. Airbrush inkjet print.**

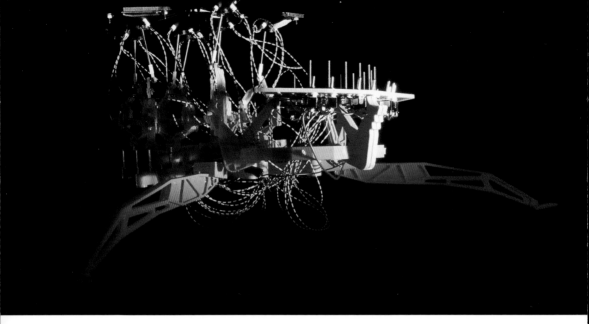

Drawing

There is a quandary for the architect trying to construct the possibility of an indeterminate condition. The conventions of architectural drawing are particularly resistant to interpretation. This is by design, to make sure that what we draw defies readings other than our own. Architectural drawing is therefore overloaded with conventions (both for the author and the reader). You might protest that this relates particularly to production drawings but the fact that the conventions allow the same thing to be understood in the same way by the many agencies that contribute to its production means that other forms of architectural representation tend to conform to the same rules. Even perspectival representation tends to be measured so that its dimensional characteristics set the terms for any other engagement. If you examine the drawn production of the most experimental architects, even those that do not build, it is very rare to find drawings that stray too far from these conventions. On the other hand, when the architect draws they do so to study or document an idea. The drawing is trying to discuss an idea while at the same time trying to avoid prescription. That sort of individual and indeterminate availability is usually achieved through interpretation. The question of interpretation is well rehearsed and broadly outside the scope of this paper. My other resistance to relying on interpretation is that once it is resolved it tends to be static, at least for each interpreter, that the life of the drawing ends with the interpretation. I am therefore looking for a way of making drawings that are available to the author for reflection and allow the reader to take possession in a way that does not rely on interpretation. I suspect that the mechanism to allow this is to look at how the drawing can become spatial, so that it requires a direct and phenomenal relationship with us.

To study how this might be achieved I have looked at two aspects. One that relates to the act of drawing, including the direct spatial relationship between the person who is drawing and what it is that they draw, a visceral or embodied relationship. The other relates to our ability to reflect on the drawing and how our position with respect to the picture plane implicates us in the content of the drawing. Again this is based on our spatial relationship to the drawing or how the drawing becomes spatial. The most useful examples of drawings that have tried to achieve this are the habitat dioramas found in natural history museums where the picture planes find an ambiguous position between material and pictorial space. I will discuss these after an introduction through three well known paintings in the National Gallery in London. I should point out that none of the examples lead to a particularly indeterminate relationship with the viewer, only the mechanism through which such a condition appears possible. Also, there is a question of the role that these drawings might play in the process of making architecture that I will address at the end. But first I will discuss our physical rela-

tionship to the drawing.

There is a convention in architectural drawings of making a distinction between the subjective, privileged by the perception of the subject, and the objective where the terms of the object (or architecture) are established independently of the subject. The implication of this is that subjective drawings such as perspectives implicate the observer or occupant and the objective drawing excludes them. I have been looking at a number of drawings that are close to the objective architectural drawing (such as the plan, section and elevation) that still implicate the viewer or author, not so much through a pictorial relationship but much more through a direct spatial dialogue. In the Capello San Servero in Naples there are two extraordinary sculptures as monuments to the patron's dead mother and father. Both are carved in marble and show a body covered in cloth. Modesty, a representation of Mary, is covered by a diaphanous veil so light and transparent it defies the heavy material from which it is made. She was carved by Corradini, who also made the maquette for the Dead Christ that was carved by Giuseppe San Martino. The representation of Mary's veil suggests an optical transparency while the Dead Christ relies on the formal transparency of the heavy shroud conforming to the topology of the body underneath. This is so articulate that it allows you to understand fragments sometimes as flesh, sometimes as fabric and sometimes something in between. If we imprinted the veil or the shroud where it touches each body, as is the idea in the image of the Turin shroud, we would have a drawing that is a normal projection but that still implicates the subject (in this case the body that makes the impression, if we imagine they were able to reflect on the image). There is a direct spatial relationship between the body and the picture plane, a folded piece of cloth.

This relationship is evident in Yves Klein's Traces of the Blue Period (Anthropométrie de l'Époque Bleue, 1960). Films [1] of the performance set up to make the paintings show him dressed in a dinner jacket and accompanied by a string quartet, orchestrating the work. Beautiful, slightly plump (as a skeletal torso would not print so well), naked female bodies are smeared with paint so that in making the painting he applies the paint to the body and the body applies it to the canvas. Some of these are simple, with a flat picture plane lying on the floor, but others have the picture

plane lying like a roll of carpet, and the partially painted body lies astride the roll separating her breasts and legs. The unfolded outcome comes much closer to the unfolded shroud, depicting a dimensionally accurate relationship between the body and (developed) space. In other words the picture plane becomes more active, or potentially critical, when folded. The relationship for those drawing is very clear, but for those viewing the painting on its own the evident 1:1 scale is critical. Normally the perspectival image presents the observer with a certain positional relationship to the represented body or object in a depth somewhere behind the canvas. The full scale of the body imprints makes the surface of the canvas active as we recognize the imprint as the thing we relate to, not through position but through scale and size. We relate to the pigment on the surface of the picture plane as a thing, in that it does not pretend to be in front or behind the picture plane. We sometimes have a similar relationship to perspectival representations of the body in panoramas where there is a full scale material foreground without any foreshortening of the scenery. In these cases any figure whose spatial location corresponds exactly with the surface of the painting will be painted full size on the canvas.

There are some early Rauschenberg drawings made by exposing ammonia blue print paper with his then wife lying on it, to produce life size photograms. In some she is still while in others she moves during the exposure. Mostly she is naked, but in one extraordinary image she weares a skirt that is diaphanous enough to allow some light to penetrate and register on the blueprint. These were made on the floor of their apartment and processed in their shower. The picture plane remained flat (on the floor) so that it does not wrap her body unless she rolls on it. These prints start to give an indication of what the prints from the shroud might be like, but without the folds. They are between perspectival and objective projection as the exposing light sometimes scans and sometimes projects from a single position. While Klein's traces are material in their painterly texture, these images are made by a photographic process that leaves a shadow that implicates a body on one or other side of the film plane. The shadow presupposes an origin and as a result makes the space between the absent figure and its shadow present. This idea is eloquently worked in Duchamp's Tu m' made in 1918. The canvas bears perspectival images (of his Standard Measure of Stoppages, for instance) that deny the plane's material presence in the normal way but is also registered materially through a tear in the cloth. The picture plane is also revealed by three shadows that are anamorphic projections of his readymades; a bicycle wheel, a corkscrew and coat hooks. These completely disregard the perspectival space represented pictorially in the painting and suggest that the origins of the shadows exist in the space behind the viewer. They land on the surface of the painting, thus denying the illusory space constructed by perspective. Each shadow is placed in space by the degree of anamorphic distortion. Typically, perspective paintings project an image that appears to lie behind the canvas . This is unusual in that it projects space the observer's side of the canvas, the domain more usually discussed in painting by the reflections in a mirror. The shadows lie on the surface of the canvas and not on the objects represented on it.

To understand the possibility of such a relationship I have been looking at photographs of drawing offices where the item that is being drawn is registered full size. In one, Harvey Earl is shown with some of his colleagues next to a drawing of the General Motors Firebird III show car (circa 1957). The car is being drawn full size on large vertical drawing boards. The show car's primary aim is to be desired, and it will be seen mostly in elevation, even for this rhetorically three-dimensional car. The drawing proposes the vehicle in this aspect and the draftsmen measure the full size drawing with their bodies, a calibration that works both for them as they work on the thing and for us observing them and it.

If we move to a photograph of the drawing office in Ford's Willow Run aeroplane factory, designed by Albert Kahn (Ypsilanti, Michigan, photographed sometime between March 1941 and December 1942) the situation has changed. The Liberator aeroplane is too large to be drawn full size in the vertical plane so a horizontal drawing board is used, where the draftsmen must lie down to draw. I would like to introduce you to some of the characters in the photograph.

Left: Drawing office at Ford's Willow Run bomber plant at Ypsilanti, Michigan. Photographed for architect Albert Kahn and Architectural Record by Hedrich Blessing, Chicago, circa 1942. Courtesy of the Chicago Historical Society, image number HB-07074-G.

Below: Eugene uses both the mattress and the protective bootees.

Eugene is a young trainee and is a model of conformity in his use of the table. He lies on a mattress to provide comfort for him and to stop his sweat from crinkling the drawing (or subverting the picture plane). On his feet he wears a pair of cute bootees. These have a similar purpose to the mattress, allowing the feet greater freedom to balance the body outside its bounds. They also protect the drawing as he moves on and off it. The image appears anamorphically to Eugene on account of his oblique view, except in the close locality beneath his face.

Left: Chuck is too proud to wear the bootees so his feet hang over the edge of the board so as not to scuff the drawing. Maybe this affects the location of what he draws.

Below: Red rel on gravity to lo his curve on th picture plane, he uses his lef hand to suppo his body while draws.

Left: Rip is proud that he does not sweat, so he does not use the mattress.

Chuck works nearby. He too uses the mattress, but is too proud to wear the bootees. Instead he still wears his shoes that would otherwise scuff the drawing if he did not leave them dangling over the edge of the board. It is easy to imagine that Chuck chooses to draw his components closer to the edge of the wing than they might ideally want to be, on account of this pride. His relationship to the picture plane is limited by his acceptance of the apparatus that allows his body licence on the board.

Rip and Red are the curve kings. Rip uses railway and French curves, like those seen in the Firebird photograph. They are independent of the inclination of the board. He is proud that he does not sweat, so he chooses not to use the mattress, his physiology allowing a closer, if less comfortable, relationship to the board. Like the Yves Klein body painters, he has a visceral relationship to his work but this time for the very reason that this relationship does not register. Red is using a weighted flexible curve, his mode of drawing dependent on gravity and the horizontality of the board (the spatial position of the board matters). Like Rip and Chuck his relationship to the image is similar to Eugene's.

Dick and Duke are somewhat older and more senior. No more gymnastics of climbing on the table for them. Dick patrols the perimeter, his

Right: **Dick patrols the perimeter and has a higher, more frontal view than the anamorphic view of the draftsmen.**

Far right: **Duke is the boss. His body penetrates the picture plane.**

standing position providing a more frontal view of proceedings compared to that of the draftsmen. Working from separate component drawings he is able to use the table as a normal desk. Duke is the foreman for this table and has a cut out within the board, giving him the most normal overview.

In this example there is still the registration of scale as they draw the aeroplane full size but the physical engagement of the draftsmen with the surface make the drawing important as a thing as well as an image. This is also true of the Klein traces, especially when they are folded. They suggest that the drawing has the capacity to be occupied as well as represented. They illustrate ways in which the drawing can bridge between material and pictorial space. In the following

section I will discuss the potential for the pictorial image constructed relative to the observer to make the same leap. Three well known works from the National gallery in London help illustrate the potential of the picture plane to become spatial beyond a purely pictorial performance.

If you view Caravaggio's painting The Supper at Emmaus (1601) from a frontal position, you will see a figure on the right hand side of the canvas with outstretched arms. His arm span is foreshortened in our view, with his left hand closest to us and his right hand

fading into the distance. This is painted with such facility that the illusion of depth is almost visceral. If he were really there, as you move over to your left you would see more of his chest, and start to see him frontally. With the painting, of course, as you make the same move you see no more of him than you did earlier. Instead your view of the painting starts to become foreshortened, but your familiarity with the frame allows your perception to compensate for this parallax. Although you see an oblique view of the painting you understand it as if from the frontal viewing position. Wher-

ever you look from, you see the same thing in pretty much the same way. The picture plane is the point of contact between two and three dimensions and the frame establishes the edge between the picture plane's space, in this case perspectival, and ours.

A few rooms away in Holbein's The Ambassadors (1533) the situation changes. As we observe the French Ambassador and the Bishop of Lavaur from the front we see a strange figure below them. As we move to the right this turns into the normal perspectival view of a human skull. While resolving this image the two portly figures become foreshortened, and you have to decide whether to compensate for parallax or understand them on the terms of the normal skull, just as you had to understand the skull

Pinhole photographs on Polaroid film looking through a model of Van Hoegstratten's peep show (with the doors cut out) into Nat Chard's studio, 2005. The pinhole camera is made with a lot of side shift to capture the full view while keeping the film plane parallel to the back wall of the peepshow.

The lighting is varied between the photographs to play on the ambiguity set up when there is a discrepancy between the space of the box and the space of the image. The light shining up through the far door lands on the ceiling of the box, which anamorphically represents a continuation of the far wall in the image. As a result the light appears to land on the very same surface that it enters through. The dark shadows in the image to the left delineate the floor and ceiling of the box.

on the terms of the men in the frontal view. The anamorphic projection of the skull requires you to have a particular spatial relationship to the painting to see it undistorted, and so your position in space starts to effect the content of the painting. Now you have a part, albeit prescribed and small, in the construction of the painting - through perception, not reading. The critical difference between this and the space in cubist painting, from a spatial point of view, is that the various positions alluded to in the cubist painting are read simultaneously while the anamorphic painting requires a duration and positional adjustment to explore it. We see the distended image and we anticipate its resolution; we resolve the image remembering what it had been. We have to move our body with respect to the painting to resolve its various parts. Much of the

pleasure of the picture lies at the seam of either resolution (normal or anamorphic). Thus anamorphism can spatialize the picture, but what of the plane?

Van Hoegstratten's peep show is a box with one open side. It has a peep hole at either end, each the origin of a perspectival view when our eye is against it. If the box were painted as a scale model of a room, with the wall of the box as a wall of a room, the ceiling of the box as the ceiling of the room and so on, you would see a perspectival view through the peephole. This is the perspectival basis of the

The difference between the space of both the box and the illusory image are clearly visible. Note again the way the light coming through the door lands on the inside of the box and on the image.

painting, in that where the floor of the box coincides with the floor of the room, the tiles are painted normally on the horizontal plane. But although there are places where the junctions of surfaces in the box and surfaces in the room coincide, such as the floor and wall at one end, there are as many conditions that do not. Objects within the space end up as anamorphic projections across the floor and continuing up the walls of the box. When viewed from the peepholes it looks completely normal, even though the condition at each end changes. When viewed from the open side (that lets in the light to see the painting) the disjunction between material and pictorial space becomes apparent. The slippage of the pictorial edge (say between floor and wall) against its material counterpart describes a strange and perplexing space that is at odds with the image we have just seen through the peephole, so that we start to question the primacy of the picture or the box. Or more interestingly perhaps, enjoy the difference between them. From these examples we can see that the picture can become available spatially through anamorphism and the plane through folding, devices familiar to us from baroque architecture. But my interest in this material is in the way it helps me understand the spatial possibilities of drawing and much less in the illusory.

A view through the opposite peephole to the previous images.

The habitat diorama is an uncanny world where stuffed animals stand on a scenographic foreground with a painted backdrop that wraps around in a curve behind and to the sides of them. The combination of these elements constructs an illusion of being there for the observer. Individually they present vast landscapes stretching out in an arc in front of the observer with distant horizons. The observer takes a few steps either side and finds them self looking at a similar expanse, although this time the view might be at another time of day or year and maybe in another continent. The panorama, a clear antecedent of the diorama, avoids these strange and wonderful folds through its autonomy. To view the spectacle (usually a land or sea battle or the view over a city painted on a 360 degree canvas) I have to climb a stair to a viewing gallery in the centre of a circular picture plane and with the more permanent installations (for many panorama paintings toured from city to city) a scenographic three-dimensional foreground. I have to climb the stair as the painting blocks any horizontal route in or out from the viewing position. The panorama differs from the framed landscape painting by having no vertical edges, as it is a cylinder. The viewing position tries to obscure the upper and lower edges, using practical elements such as the balustrade and the reflectors that evenly distribute the daylight over the painting. So whichever

Alaska Brown Bear, Belmore Browne, 1941
Hall of North American Mammals, American
Museum of Natural History, New York. Stere-
oscopic pair.

way I look I see the landscape. It does not only have a pictorial likeness to the place, as in the framed painting, but it is more like being there. As I turn around I see what I might see if I had been there at the moment that the view recollects. The panorama implicates me, the observer, in its spatial construction. The diorama also tries to implicate me but with the compromise that comes from packing many more views into a given space than might be possible with panoramas. If we cut a panorama in half we get much of the spatial effect of being there without the need to enter by a staircase, as one side is now open (or glazed).

The first habitat diorama was the Biological Museum in Uppsala built in 1889 in what had formerly been an anatomical theatre. It was made by Gustaf Kolthoff, a Swedish naturalist and marksman who noticed that the birds and animals he shot were not as interesting when stuffed as they were when alive. [2] He realized that one reason for this was that many of their characteristics related to their environment, and

Pine For-
ames Perry
h, 1955
can Mu-
of Natural
y, New

by placing them in a representation of that place he hoped that they would once again regain their interest. He subsequently built the Biological Museum in Stockholm (1893) that is a hybrid of several dioramas of Scandinavian scenes seamlessly stitched into a panorama. You enter from below into a two story viewing cabin that is glazed all round. The problematic relationship with the horizon on the upper level (to view flying and nesting birds) is not resolved. On the lower level the wonderful painted backdrop by Bruno Liljefors (who also worked on the diorama at Uppsala) is broken by scenic elements such as cliffs and hills. The critical difference between

these paintings and those in the panorama is that in the latter the construction of the painting is based very closely on the position of the observer. The angle of view that I would have had over the landscape (had I been there for the represented event) is the same as the angle of view I have of the panorama. Of course, if this were not the case the panorama would not work as the view would either end too soon leaving a gap in the canvas where the two ends of the

Coyote, James
Perry Wilson, 1949
Hall of North
American Mammals,
American Museum
of Natural History,
New York.

painting should join, or conversely, the ends of the painting would overlap each other. For this explanation I imagine the painting as a ribbon whose two vertical ends should meet and match exactly to form a cylinder. In Liljefors' paintings there appears to be a much looser construction, based on the conventions of framed landscape paintings. In this paper I will discuss the importance of registering the location of the viewer as a way of spatialising the picture plane but first I will describe some of the ways in which the diorama engages the observer with the landscape.

During the nineteen twenties, thirties and forties, the American Museum of Natural History (AMNH) in New York engaged in an ambitious diorama building program. The aim was similar to that of the Biological Museum in Stockholm, but on a much greater scale, to exhibit the animals of the world in a series of contexts that would make sense of them. There are early examples in the Asian mammals gallery that reveal some of the early techniques to register a perspectival view on a curved surface. The work is accomplished but pales when compared to the later Hall of African Mammals (also known as the Akeley African Hall), or the high point of diorama construction, the North American Mammals hall. The dioramas were expensive to build, not only in terms of production but also in the

Mule Deer, James
Perry Wilson, 1943
Hall of North
American Mammals,
American Museum of
Natural History, New
York.

research and surveys that went into them, and benefactors had to be found to fund them. The expeditions involved photographic and painted surveys made at the site, along with collections of plant material and earth and rock samples. The focus of the dioramas is on the animals and these were also shot and skinned on the expeditions. Photographs of these trips show the diorama painters standing at their easels under improvised sunshades. But there was also a very macho side to the hunting, and one shot shows Carl Akeley, his arm in a sling, standing next to a leopard strung up by its hind legs after he had killed it with his bare hands. But Akeley's motivation for these activities was also an awareness of the danger to the animal populations "Two hundred years from now naturalists and scientists will find in such museum exhibits as African Hall the only existent records of some of the animals which today we are able to photograph and study in their forest environment". *[3]*

In March 1942 Alfred Parr became director of the museum, moving from the Yale Peabody Museum of Natural History, with a mandate to develop exhibits that were less expensive than the dioramas. Parr's diagnosis was as follows: "These groups have become large and expensive, and have probably reached their ultimate artistic perfection. What is now realized is that they have become ends

Libyan Desert, James
Perry Wilson, 1939
Akeley Hall of African
Mammals, American
Museum of Natural His-
tory, New York.

in themselves. The beauty of the composition and not the natural history content is what the visitor sees. It has been suggested that such groups are 95% art and 5% science. It has been considered justifiable to use 95% art, if by that means only 5% of science could be put over, but many are skeptical". There are many contributors to this art, from the foreground artists and taxidermists such as Ralph Morrill to the background painters such as Francis Lee Jaques, who painted exquisite though not always perspectively precise birds in his scenes, or the operatic work of Belmore Browne.

Browne trained at the New York School of Art and was a distinguished landscape painter as well as diorama artist. Another, William R. Leigh trained in Munich and it was under his guidance that James Perry Wilson worked for a while as an apprentice. Wilson progressively developed a rigorous projective geometry for dioramas that I will describe later and painted some of the finest examples. J.P.Wilson studied architecture at Columbia University, graduating in 1914 and worked as an architect for twenty years, principally in the office of Bertrum Goodhue where he concentrated on perspective drawings. Goodhue said of Wilson "If I want the shadow of an irregularly-curved angular body cast on an irregularly-shaped surface, from a certain angle and from a certain distance at a time of day on a certain day of the year, I ask Mr. Wilson to do this thing, and lo! And behold! After many days, the result is accomplished and no one, I less than any, questions the accuracy of the result." Wilson's employment as a diorama painter started with a chance meeting with an employee of the AMNH who encouraged him to show his paintings to James L. Clark, the director of diorama construction (Anderson 2000). His first works are in the Akeley African Hall where he worked to William R. Leigh's field studies. The colour range in these African dioramas is noticeably golden, more consistent with Leigh's work than Wilson's later dioramas, with their iridescent blues.

The development of taxidermy at the AMNH developed along with the painting techniques, as did the foreground artistry. The history of these is well documented elsewhere and I don't want to dwell on it except where it compliments the ideas set up by the backgrounds; where they contribute to the phenomenal sense of being there. In the animals this took a step forward with the development of rigid armatures for the animals; instead of stuffing (or upholstering as it has been unkindly called) the skins are bonded to well formed armatures that are a little like ércoché figures, the skeleton and musculature without the skin. The positioning of the animals in the diorama groups interests me in two ways; their social groupings, or how they relate spatially to one another and the observer and the way they relate to the topography. In Belmore Browne's Osborn Caribou group two of the animals look at you so that you become implicated as a potential predator. One surveys the landscape to the left (and thereby inviting you to do the same) while another looks for a possible escape route. The fifth continues eat-

ing. The scene is reminiscent of the Robert Doisneau photograph of Daniel Pipard painting on the Pont des Arts where the painter obscures his subject sitting on a bench so that it is hard to ratify the nude woman in his painting. One is drawn to ponder this by the observer, who compares the painting with the view. As if this has not established enough depth in the composition, the observer's dog looks back at the photographer, or more importantly you, the observer. [5] Or maybe Velazquez's famous Las Meninas where we, as the viewers of the painting, also find ourselves as the subject of the artist shown in the painting, our position confirmed in a mirror on the far wall. The assembly of animals not only locates the anthropological role of the animals to each other and their strategic relationship to the territory but also their relationship to you. Compositionally this helps include you in the depth of the work and ground the animals in the scene. The spatiality of the scene is supported by the poise of the animals. In another Browne group, the White Sheep, one animal looks at you while the other two take in other parts of the scenery, again inviting you to do the same. Wilson's Wapiti group has the animals all facing the same direction with the furthest female turning towards

you as if taken by surprise, while the foreground male warns you off. This group is traversing a rolling hillside, the articulacy of their muscles describing the work they have to do and their relation to the ground. This anatomical precision helps describe their phenomenal relationship to the topography, exaggerated in Wilson's Jaguar or Grizzly Bear dioramas. (p.57) The same attention to detail and subtle observation can be seen in the foreground work, where in the Mule Deer group there are slight changes in the scree where the animals habitually walk.

In Jaques' Walrus group in the Ocean Life hall the walruses duly talk to each other, to us and to the scenery. I was a little disappointed in the snow, however. I was taken round the Copenhagen Zoological museum by one of the taxidermists. When we came to their walrus diorama he let slip dark taxidermist jokes about the shooting, skinning and mounting of these animals, a process he had been fully involved in. What he was most proud of, however, was the representation of urine and excrement on the snow. He explained how evident their lack of hygiene had been to him when he was deciding which ones to shoot. I subsequently visited the Stockholm Natural History museum, and their walrus diorama had even more visceral faeces, not just their smears on the snow. This Scandinavian sensibility for cleanliness and hygiene had

, James
Wilson,

North
can Mam-
American
um of
al History,
'ork.

clearly been lost on the Americans, however, as the snow in Jaques version is spotless.

These observations relate to the physical elements of the scene and to some extent how sense is made of the join between the physical and the pictorial. I will now move on to the part that interests me most, the painted background. The shell of the diorama is curved so as to be able to contain the animals. If there was a flat painting behind the animals it would have to be very large if it was to absorb your whole view and its frame would be behind the animals, encouraging a separation between the physical and the pictorial.

In a paper on diorama techniques in the Museum News [6] F.L.Jaques outlines what he sees as the principle problems of background painting "In the technical use of the background the problem of the horizon is always the first consideration, For a group with a curved background the horizon should be at eye level. Since we are not all the same height this is obviously impossible, therefore a figure which represents a compromise must be determined. If the observer's eye is lower than the horizon, the horizon will appear to bend up at the corners; if the eye is above, the corners or sides will appear to bend down. About five feet is probably the most satisfactory solution." He later carries on

Left: J.P. Wilson's sky color test for Grizzly Bear group (and other dioramas at the AMNH) Collection and with kind permission of Ruth Morrill.

Right: Grizzly Bear, James Perry Wilson, 1941 Hall of North American Mammals, American Museum of Natural History, New York.

"If we draw squares representing a painting on a long, rectangular, flat surface, and bend this surface to represent a curved background, it will appear and photograph, as in plate III Fig. 1; when viewed from the normal observer's position. This is obviously unsatisfactory, though we often accept it without question. What we want is an image that will be represented by true squares on the plane occupied by the glass front. If then, we project a pattern of true squares on to the curved background from the viewpoint of the eye, we get a distorted pattern, which if laid flat, would be as shown in Plate III fig 2. If this is bent into the shape of a background again, and photographed from the point at which it was projected, it will appear on the plate as true squares.

However, this result, while entirely satisfactory as far as the camera is concerned, would still not be entirely satisfactory to the eye, which has accustomed itself to viewing pictures from an angle; and no matter how successful the back-

ground may be, it still remains a picture. The eye compensates somewhat for the distorted image that it sees. Inversely, an image drawn with some distortion is likely to appear so even if it would photograph correctly from the same viewpoint."

"Obviously the correct angle from which to view any point of a background is the perpendicular. A little study will show, however, that it is impossible from any position outside the case front to view some parts of a normally shaped background from the perpendicular. ...The lesson to be drawn from this is simply that we must not consider a curved background as a long flat normal picture bent into that shape. Horizontal or near horizontal lines should be avoided as much as possible toward the sides of the painting. Where they must be used they should be drawn up as they approach the sides, if they be below the horizon, and down if they be above. The deviation can be easily determined by placing a horizontal stick at the plane of the glass and sighting it from the nor-

Black Bear, James Perry
Wilson, 1947
Hall of North American
Mammals, American
Museum of Natural His-
tory, New York.

mal viewpoint".

I include such a long section as
it exemplifies the techniques of
diorama painting before Wilson.
As you can understand from
Goodhue's remarks that I quoted
earlier, Wilson worked with tremendous precision, not only in
terms of geometry but in terms of
the other aspects that would give
the view meaning, the time of day
and year for example. He was dis-
satisfied with the approximations
used by his colleagues. William R.
Leigh left soon after Wilson's ar-
rival, leaving him to develop the
art and science of diorama paint-

ing beyond any other.

The Jaques quotation outlines a technique for
transferring a flat picture plane onto a curved
surface, a pictorial approach. Wilson was not
prepared to accept the compromises outlined
by Jaques and started to develop his own survey and projection methods based on a more
phenomenological approach. The painters took
photographs and made paintings on the site. Although Wilson goes on at length about his admi-
ration for Kodachrome reversal (slide) film in his
letters [7], the colour rendering and tonal range
did not describe the site accurately enough, so
he would depend on his paintings to cover these
aspects. He would rely on the photographs to
generate the geometry. To overcome the problems outlined by Jaques he photographed pan-

White Rhinoceros,
James Perry Wilson,
1937
Akeley Hall of
African Mammals,
American Museum
of Natural History,
New York.

oramas. He would take a central shot and then two or three either side, usually with a 35mm focal length lens on a 35mm camera, though sometimes with a 50mm lens. By rotating the camera on a tripod head set at five foot two inches above the ground, and carefully registering the limits of each frame, he would construct a series that could be joined up. Technically this gave him a facetted picture plane (for in each photograph the film is located in the camera as a flat surface) like five faces of an octagon perhaps. This was further developed with photographs above and below each facet to capture the sky and the ground, or foreground. In order to relate this to the diorama shell he made two moves, one to convert this faceted picture plane into a semi circular one and another to project that onto the diorama shell geometry. To ac-

complish the first he calculated grids that could be overlaid on the slides to make this compensation, both for the horizontal and inclined photographs. The size of the grid for the slide would depend on the size of grid he wanted to use on the diorama shell [8], giving him a cylindrical picture plane. So why, when he starts out with a faceted spherical picture plane from his photographs (the assembly of those that establish the horizon along with the sky and foreground ones set at the angle from which they were photographed) does he move to a two dimensional curve (the part cylinder) when he

Coast Redwood Forest, James Perry Wilson 1957
American Museum of Natural History, New York.

Computer
models of
Bog Camera
casing.

will have to transfer it back to the partly spherical picture plane of the diorama shell? I think there are two principle answers to this. One is simply that the predominant area of the shell has vertical walls. The second is that his method does not require the image to be drawn at this stage. It is held as an abstract transfer grid, so as long as the projection technique that transferred the cylindrical picture plane onto the diorama shell was accurate, the nature of the intermediate (cylindrical) plane did not matter. For a full description of Wilson's grid and transfer techniques see *A Dual Grid System for Diorama Layout* by Ruth Morrill *[9]* who worked as his assistant on some of his work at the Peabody. The most important point to make about Wilson's system of transferring the photographic panorama to the diorama shell is that like the panorama, it exactly relates that angle of view of the observer on the original site to your angle of view of the diorama (given that you are standing in a normal position to the diorama). In essence, you are implicated spatially in the diorama.

This is a good moment to discuss the shape of the shell. One consideration is economy, the need to construct the illusion of endless horizons into the smallest possible space that would accept the animals to be displayed. All the other factors battle against this. The spatial idea is to present the most unbounded view, so that al-

Bog Camera
components.

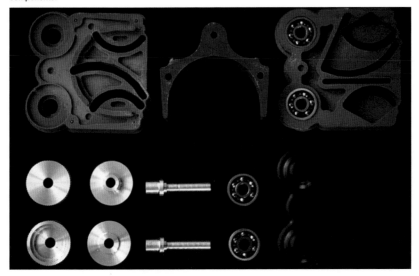

though you are looking into an internal room of say three or four metres depth it might seem as though you are looking out to the horizon. This is the illusory aim. To construct this illusion there are a number of elements, the material foreground and the pictorial background, a frame to limit the viewing position and electric lighting. The painted background has two levels of performance; the pictorial representation of the scene that is the subject matter that dominates this paper and the material shell, that supports the paint. I will discuss the techniques of trying to make the painting as transparent as possible later. The form of the shell is curved in plan and in section so that it does not reveal any corners or sharp folds, the elements that would register the surface in space. In addition to beeing curved in plan, as in the panorama, the diorama shell is curved in section to deny a transition between wall and ceiling. There are various techniques for dealing with the tie-in, the junction between the material scenery and the pictorial background that I will lead on to. The nature of the geometric adjustments that Jaques talks about, and that are perfected by Wilson, cause anamorphic distortions to the sides of the diorama image, the parts of the surface that return towards the viewing window. The deeper the diorama in relation to its width, the greater its anamorphism. This sets up a paradox that the greater the actual depth, the harder it be-

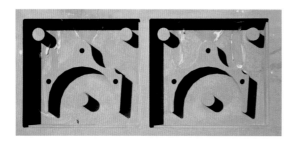

Patterns, moulds and components for Bog Camera.

comes to represent illusory depth. The economics of museum hall building therefore conspire to make the shallow curve the most common diorama shape. Although the half lozenge is sometimes used, a continuous curve of varying radii avoids the conspicuous transition between a curved and flat surface in plan. In section, the walls are normally vertical until the scenery has all turned to sky. This is the first point where the material and pictorial touch each other, for if the surface is getting close to you and what is painted on the surface is receding, your perception is put in a quandary. Imagine, for instance, a mountain scene where the summit is the furthest land object from the viewer. If it is painted on the part of the backdrop that starts to fold forwards, cyclorama like, towards the viewer, your registration of the paint in space tells you that the summit is getting closer to you while your experience of mountains and the perspective tells you that it is receding. Furthermore, if you view the scene from either side of a normal, frontal position, the mountain summit will be distorted by the curve, not only appearing to droop towards you but bend to one side, like a banana. To avoid this, most land scenery is kept to the vertical section with the sky crossing the transition between vertical and the curved return. Many of the painters, Browne and Wilson in particular, enjoyed their skies and the amorphous nature of the clouds could cope with

Bog Camera
with and
without
casing.

Bog Camera
top view.

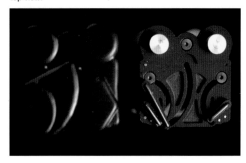

such distortion or ambiguous location. In some situations this strategy is not possible, for example in forests, where the whole shell is painted with trees. In Wilson's Black Bear group in the North American hall he paints distortions in the tree trunks at the transition between vertical and curve so as to disguise the banana effect, and tries to obscure the trunks with leaves and branches. These have a secondary effect that they are coming towards the viewer in both form (the shape of the shell) and illusory perspective. In the Okapi group in the African hall a separate canopy is installed and painted with leaves so that the junction between the trunk and the ceiling return could be disguised. The geometric precision of tree trunks makes them a particularly hard subject. The extreme example of this is in Wilson's forced perspective of Californian redwoods in the Forestry hall, the Coast Redwood forest group (p. 58-59). The diorama is seven feet deep and represents a two hundred and seventy foot depth before the painting begins, although the material closest to the viewer is full size. To achieve this every bracken leaf has to be made both to work in perspectival depth and positional anamorphism. The diorama is tall and thin, partly due to the subject matter, but also to limit the viewpoint, so critical in forced perspective and much more so than in most dioramas. [10] The least convincing point is where the middle ground tree trunks meet the

Bog Camera
Rear view.

Bog Camera
three quarter
view.

sky and have to be disguised by clumps of foliage. At the Yale Peabody, Wilson's Mountain Sheep group is sited in a wedge shaped corner, where the long side of the wedge that progressively comes towards the viewer represents a mountain valley receding into the distance. Although he does not have to contend with a change of curve as well (as in the transition between ceiling and wall) it is still a tricky problem. Despite these unpromising circumstances, with the material shell contradicting the illusion in the perspective, the group remains one of the outstanding dioramas, a testament

not only to Wilson's facility but also to his projection method to which I will now return.

The typical diorama shell therefore has curved walls and a domed ceiling, with continually changing radius points. Jaques method of approximating the perspective around the horizon and eyeballing it with the help of a horizontal sighting rod positioned on the viewing plane's horizon provides the basis for accomplished scenographic paintings. Wilson's analysis of how to push the sense of being there can be divided into a number of categories. They are not documented by him as ideas, in fact hardly documented by him at all, but have to be deduced from his actions. We have looked at his first move, to see the picture plane panoramically and not pictorially, so that the viewer may

turn their head and not lose the ideal viewing point. He then had to transfer this panorama onto the shell, and where we left it he had made an intermediate picture plane, a curved negotiator between the faceted picture plane of the photographs and the variable geometry of the diorama shell.

In a letter to Thanos Johnson *[11]*, Wilson explained it like this "As for your comments on producing the effect of space in the backgrounds; there is no magical formula for this... As you know I usually paint studies in the field and take a series of overlapping photographs covering the entire panorama. In transferring these to the background, the first consideration of importance is establishing the scale of the background, so that from the normal view-

point (about two feet in front of the glass) objects will appear lifesize (that is they will cover the same visual angle that they did in the actual scene). To produce this effect, the size of an object in the background must be to its size in the slide, as the distance from the eye to the wall is to the focal length of the lens with which the photograph was taken. For example, suppose the distance from the eye to the wall is ten feet (120 inches); and the slides were taken with 35mm lenses (standard for stereo lenses); and suppose further that you have applied to the slide a grid with squares of 1/10

inch. 35Mm = 1 3/8 inch or 11/8 inch, then the squares in the grid on the wall must be 120 divided by 11/8 x 1/10 or 8 and 8/11th inches. Is that clear? The grids for the slides must be adjusted to convert the perspective from plane to cylindrical; and the grid for the wall must be adjusted according to the shape of the background so that from a normal viewing point the squares will all appear true and equal. This will insure correct perspective when seen from the normal viewing point."

This geometric construction relies on an old perspectival conceit, that the viewer is a cyclops. Of course the foreground is three dimensional, but the surface of the shell is a problem, for if you register an item on it then you register the plane. In the Berlin Natural History Museum, for example, careful foregrounds are negated by painterly backgrounds, the expression of the brushstroke registering the picture plane as a distinct surface. The diorama painter's ideal (as for the realist landscape painter) was for their picture plane to be transparent, to disappear as a surface. Wilson and several of his colleagues were careful with their brushstrokes and the use of medium, especially in the areas where the diorama lighting might be reflected. One technique that dissolves the picture plane is stereoscopy. The illusion given by left

est shot
...og Camera
...penhagen
...ur, similar
...o the one
...e left. Note
...amor-
...distortion
...d to create
...age of an
...led dio-
...(compare
...at picture
on left).

and right eye images constructs a three dimensional space, removing the surface of the picture plane altogether. Wilson experimented with stereoscopic photography, and this provided the component of his surveys that he considered the closest to being there. He would use them when he was painting. Comparing his work after he started using these, to before, or compared to the work of his colleagues, the greatest difference I can see is in his shadow detail. Insects are often studied using stereoscopic photography as it separates the thing from its surroundings, even in confused micro undergrowths. If you study below the branches at the edge of a forest in many landscape paintings and dioramas you often see a general shadow with the outside tree trunks painted and then a confu-

sion of marks to suggest the trees within. In Wilson's post stereoscopic work the detail within the forest is painted with just as much precision as everywhere else (taking into account the progressive haze as the landscape recedes). In his Jeffrey Pine Forrest diorama (p.48) in the North American Forests Hall there is a section to the right of the foreground (full size and three dimensional) tree trunk that depicts a view deep into the forest. The quality of light is partly responsible for the sense of depth in here. Wilson, like many landscape painters mixed all his hues

Panorama assembled out of J.P.Wilson's survey photographs of the Cold Bog site in Connecticut, taken on June 17th 1949. Photograph by J.P.Wilson, by kind courtesy of Ruth Morrill.

from a limited range of primary and secondary coloured oil paints [12] and used no blacks - but the detail that allows you to spatially separate one tree from another comes, I believe, from his use of stereoscopic photography. Photographic film does not have the same capacity to deal with tonal range as the human eye, and this is precisely the sort of place where a single photograph would confuse, and where the detail would be hard to pin down on a plein air painting. I believe that you can see the effect also in some of the delicious painting of transparency and reflection through water. If you compare the Coyote group (p.50) in the North American hall with his White Rhinoceros group (p.59) in

the African hall, both sets of water are beautifully painted. But in the latter he depended on other people's survey information and the pool lacks the depth exhibited in the Coyote group.

I had another theory as to why he might have used stereoscopy, one that is almost certainly not the case, although it is so clearly related to the issue of the junction of material and pictorial space that I will relate it anyway. The mechanism of stereoscopic vision is well

understood, in that the difference between the view from each eye provides the triganomic information to precisely locate something in space, so that we might pick it up and bring it to our mouths, for instance, or we might catch a flying ball. Our eyes are typically 65mm apart, centre-to-centre. When we take stereo photographs we can take them with this separation, the strategy of many proprietary 3D cameras. If we do this to take a close up of the insects I mentioned earlier, it is a little like

asking us to go cross eyed, the separation with respect to the distance to the object is too great so it strains our eyes. Much better results are obtained with a smaller separation. If we take a 3D photograph of New York from the top of the Empire State building with 65mm separation the image will appear quite flat. If we separate the two images by several meters we will get tremendous depth. The rule of thumb to get a good clear stereoscopic separation in depth is to make the separation between lens centres one thirtieth of the distance to the object. My point is related to what 3D photographers refer to as stereo acuity. *[13]* In theory we are able to perceive depth through stereoscopic vision

(with the 65mm separation of our eyes) up to a distance of 6km (3.73 miles) and down to a distance of two inches. The former distance is called stereo infinity. In practice air currents and temperature vari- ations seriously reduce this distance. For our purposes the optimal depth effect is at two metres and this is halved at four metres. By three metres an observer with typical eyesight can pick out depth distances above 10mm, or just under half an inch. This falling off of stereo acu-

Right: Ruth Morrill, who worked with J.P.Wilson on some of his later dioramas and Wilson scholar Michael Anderson at the Cold Bog site in Connecticut on June 17th 2001, fifty two years to the day after the original survey. Three of the Bog cameras are seen in the foreground. To achieve good stereoscopic results between the photographs it is important that they have the same horizon, a tricky problem when the tripods are on a floating raft of sphagnum moss.

Left: Bog camera photograph of Cold Bog site in Connecticut, June 17th 2001. Note how anamorphic adjustment of the image flattens the horizon compared to the normal photograph. If this photograph was folded into the shape of the bog diorama shell and you viewed it from the normal viewing position you would resolve the image as if you were on the site where the photograph were taken.

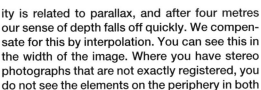

Right: Cold Bog site with normal (flat film plane) camera reveals the horseshoe rim of trees rising around the bog, June 17th 2001.

KOD/AK E100   6ʔ

ity is related to parallax, and after four metres our sense of depth falls off quickly. We compensate for this by interpolation. You can see this in the width of the image. Where you have stereo photographs that are not exactly registered, you do not see the elements on the periphery in both shots (or in both eyes), but these sections do not appear as flat. In your peripheral vision the same thing happens. Although some of the view is excluded from one eye, by your nose for instance,

your brain assembles a continuously three-dimensional sense
of the world. In depth a similar
thing happens, so that as stereoscopic vision fails you assemble
the stereoscopic information with

other mechanisms such as a perspectival understanding of depth. When you look at a three
dimensional photograph and close one eye,
then open it again, it becomes clear where the
(depth) threshold between stereoscopy and perspective lies. If I were to construct a diorama,

Left: Bog camera photograph of Cold Bog diorama the Yale Peabody Museum of Natural History, June 18th 2001. This photograph accurately unpeels the diorama's painted background, as if it were taken off its shell and hung flat on a wall.

Below: Cold Bog diorama at the Yale Peabody Museum of Natural History photographed with a normal (flat film plane) camera, taken June 18th 2001.

Top: Original site survey photograph on Kodachrome slide with Wilson grid superimposed. These are scratched onto a separate layer of transparent plastic. One he had drawn his grid on the diorama shell he would translate the image in charcoal while checking the slide (with grid) through a viewer.

this would seem to be the ideal place to transfer from the three-dimensional to the pictorial, at the point where stereoscopy is no longer so important. The point seems so obvious that it is annoying there is no evidence to suggest Wilson worked with this. In fact all the evidence points the other way, that where I have seen both the photographs and the diorama the junction between two and three dimensional representation happens at completely different depths in the dioramas

Full size picture plane surveyed by ten cameras that are exposed simultaneously . The selective use of some of the cameras' flashes cast anamorphic human shadows on the adjustable folded picture plane for other cameras (with their flashes switched off) to witness.

To the left:
Crane and picture plane setup prior to recording.

Below: Frame 12, camera 10. View from one of the battery of cameras seen on the right in view from camera 7.

Frame 12, camera 7, plan view. Note the simultaneous flashes from the row of cameras on the right.

from the collapse of depth in the photographs. An opportunity lost, I believe.

In an unpublished interview with fellow diorama artists Rudy Freund and Rudy Zallinger, Wilson stated "I find it (stereoscopic photography) especially valuable in foreground work, that is foreground painting. The three dimensional photograph explains so much better than the two-dimensional photograph. Working from them is the next best thing to working from nature itself. So I always take the bulk of my pictures in 3D". [14]

Beyond the geometrical precision involved in transferring the view onto the shell there are a number of other aspects that Wilson progressed. Wilson painted landscapes long before he started as a diorama painter. He had no formal training as an artist, but he spent most of his vacations in places like Westchester County, New York; Towaco, New Jersey; Pownal, Vermont and spent eighteen summers between 1919 and 1940 on Monhegan Island Maine. He was preoccupied with astronomy, meteorology and the physics of light and although his fascination with these things sometimes appears pedantic (once he wrote to Thanos Johnson who had painted the moon incorrectly "now about the crescent moon. I really am surprised at you for painting the moon at eventide in that position! You have only one possible out; it would be

Frame 12, camera 5. Note crane to adjust picture plane.

Frame 12, camera 9.

Frame 12, camera 8.

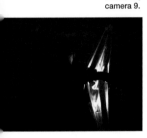

correct in the south Temperate Zone, but I don't believe you were there.") But this precision also allows his paintings to hold meaning through the coincidence and consequence of one thing on another; that the sort of sky effects the light and the lighting of the landscape and the stuffed animals for instance. This can be seen very clearly in the Wapiti group and the Jaguar diorama in the North American hall. He was instrumental in the AMNH choosing to use fluorescent lighting for their dioramas along with tungsten spots to give a better colour temperature balance. In his Libyan Desert group in the African hall he paints the scene with a low sun, picking out detail in the otherwise featureless sand topography. This posed a problem for lighting the diorama. If there was a low lighting position, it would be hard to disguise the light source and not have shadows from the animals on the painted background. To overcome this he painted the area that joins the three dimensional part of the diorama occupied by the animals as if in the shade of a dune, and balanced the warm light of the low sun with the tungsten lighting and the cool shadow to the fluorescent. Unfortunately the lighting has been rearranged to get more light on some of the animals (not the case in older photographs of the group) leaving real shadows on the ground that contradict those that he painted on the background. Although this gives a Marienbad [15] like surreality to

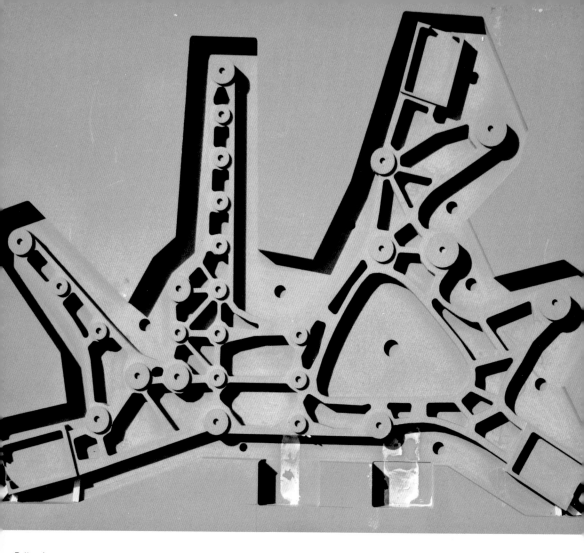

Pattern in Cibatool for the night time drawing instrument chassis.

the scene, it undoes a lot of careful thinking as to how to embody the experience of the desert in the diorama.

He was equally meticulous with his clouds, something that he knew a lot about and his general care with skies gives a tremen-

dous sense of time. While working on the Shoreline Diorama in the Yale Peabody he wrote to a friend [16] "Do you remember the cirrus clouds in the Mule Deer sky?" (The Mule Deer group is in the North American hall at the AMNH, p.51) "Well I am now at work on cirrus clouds to make those look childish. I really think they are going to have better character. Having tried painting them over the blue with colour thinned way

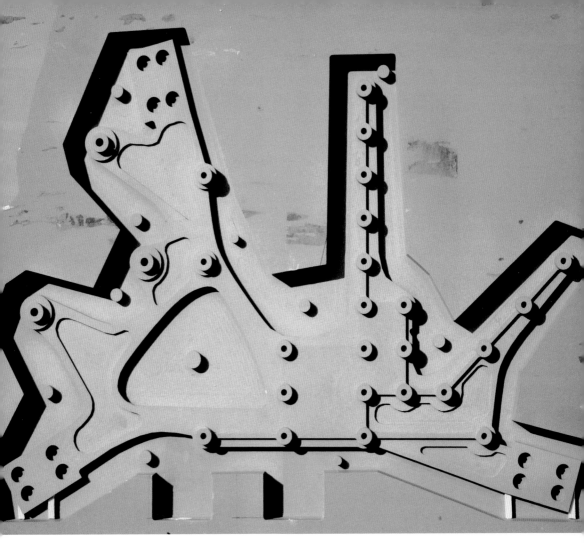

down with turpentine, I have given that method up in favour of using the colour full strength, but with very little on the brush. By rubbing this over the stippled sky, you get a light scumble, almost a dusting, of colour on the high spots, with the blue showing through between. You can control the density very exactly, and can get effects of extreme delicacy and subtlety. For colour I am using the sky colour mixed with white. Even the

densest part of the cirrus cloud is so thin that you can feel a lot of cloud through it."

After transferring the image from the gridded photographs to the shell, Wilson would start with the sky and then move down from the horizon, matching his landscape

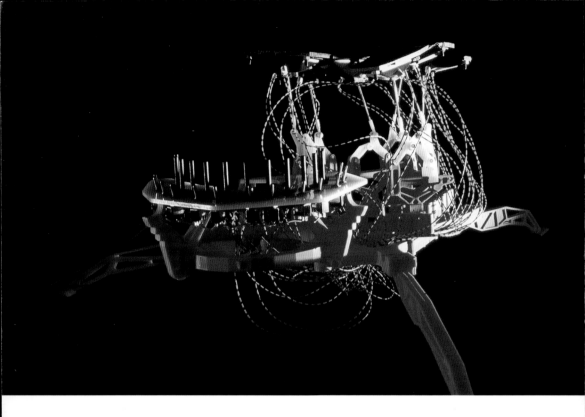

tones with that of the sky. "A typical fair weather sky, especially at high altitudes, graduates smoothly from a deep blue (Cobalt or Ultramarine) overhead, to a clear and much lighter blue, usually of a turquoise hue, at perhaps, one quarter of the distance from the horizon to the zenith (p.56). Below this level the tone usually lightens still more, but the blue colour is modified by a ground haze. The hue may be somewhat greenish, in very clear weather, or purplish, on hazy days, especially at low altitudes. These three tones-upper part of the sky, clear turquoise band, and horizon colour may be considered the key colours for the entire sky. If they are carefully prepared, all the intermediate tones may be obtained automatically by mixing these. This will insure a smooth, even graduation". [17]

Wilson used all these techniques to establish as close to a phenomenal sense of being there as he was able, both in terms of projective geometry and an understanding of the art of painting. The emphasis on the phenomenal is exemplified in the Elk diorama. He wrote to Thanos Johnson " With a 24" x 36" (projected) image on the screen, the moon's diameter is three and an eighth inches (the same as the moon painted on the Elk group background)". Taking into account Wilson's cardboard slide mounts a simple calculation indicates he was using a 300mm lens. [18]

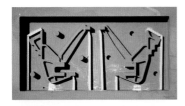

Left and below: Cibatool patterns for bracket and sub frame of night time drawing instrument.

Below: **Assembly of drawing instruments. Airbrush and pencil.**

By his normal calculation this would make the distance from the observer to the painted moon on the shell of the Elk (Wapiti) diorama (p.54,55) twenty-five feet, when in reality the distance is a little less than nineteen feet. The moon in the Elk group is only just over its own diameter above the horizon and with a difference in line with perceptual adjustments for the moon illusion [19] and Wilson's grasp of perception and astronomy it is reasonable to assume that this accounts for the difference. The moon illusion does not register dimensionally in photographs, so if he had used the moon in his survey shots it would have appeared too small.

To understand Wilson's projective geometry I designed a camera that could make all his calculations in one photograph. Three cameras were made so that I could make stereoscopic photographs (the width of the camera was such that two cameras could make accurate stereoscopic photographs of the diorama) and have a backup in case of failure in the field. The cameras are specific to Wilson's Cold Bog diorama in the Yale Peabody Museum of Natural History and use a pinhole to provide the depth of field to cope with the curved film plane. The pinhole is placed in the scale position of the ideal viewpoint, and in front of the diorama it is located at the viewpoint. When photographing the original site the camera produces

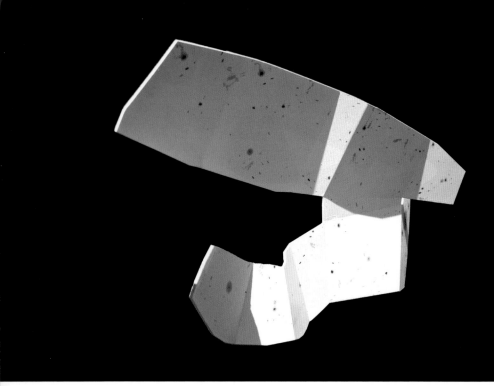

an unfolded image of the diorama
shell. When photographing the
diorama the images show an accurate unfolding of the painting.
Wilson scholar Michael Anderson
from the Yale Peabody Museum
arranged for the diorama glass to
be opened up for me and for ac-
cess to the original site in Connecticut. Fifty-two years to the day
after the original survey (under-
taken on June 17th 1949) he and
Ruth Morrill, who assisted Wilson
in some of his late work, accompanied me and helped to find the
original survey viewpoint on the
site. The nature of the place, a
sphagnum moss bog, made set-

ting up the cameras interesting, as one tripod
would move on a raft of moss as the next was
set up. Comparing my cameras' photographs
with normal views of either the site or the diorama show the anamorphic distortion required
to register the image on the curved shell. Comparing my cameras shots of the site and from
the diorama, despite half a century of growth,
reveals the precision of Wilson's technique.

You might ask what the diorama has to do with
a condition of indeterminacy. As a form of representation it tries hard to tell a precise story
and goes to great lengths to achieve a perceptual realism to determine its content. I could
try and persuade you that there are aspects of
the uncanny, as revealed in Sugimoto's black
and white photographs of some of the AMNH

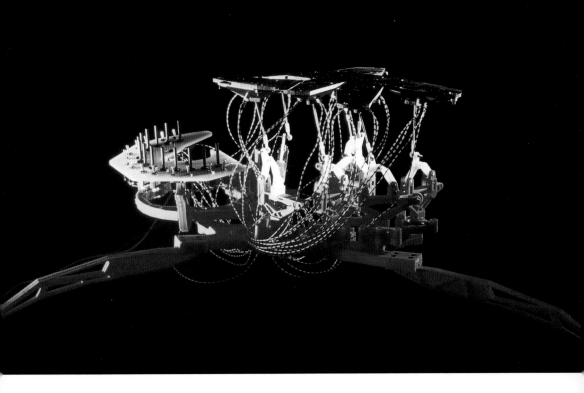

ght time
awing
trument.

groups that leave us uncertain about the status of these works. Or I could talk about the strange folds between neighbouring dioramas where you slide almost seamlessly from one climate or continent to another. But the real potential lies not in the image but in its construction. The assembly of image and space and the way the pictorial and material refer to each other promise a potential for architectural drawings to implicate the observer in their content. To illustrate such a potential I would like to remind you of the photograph Deckard finds in a drawer in Leon's apartment at the start of his search for replicants in the film Blade Runner (1982). [20]

When he analyses the image he is looking at a room reminiscent of that in Van Hoegstratten's peepshow displayed on his computer screen.

He unravels the plot by navigating a flat picture plane almost as if it is normal space. What appears to be a zoom turns out to be a dolly move into the next room. The relationship between the far mirror and the intermediate door frame reveals this parallactic shift. As he moves into the image he discovers a woman (Zhora) lying down, reflected in the mirror. To understand the construction of this image I extracted sequential frames from a tracking shot of her. She does not move - we are after all looking at a still photograph. On the left of the image is Zhora. We are looking down on her as she

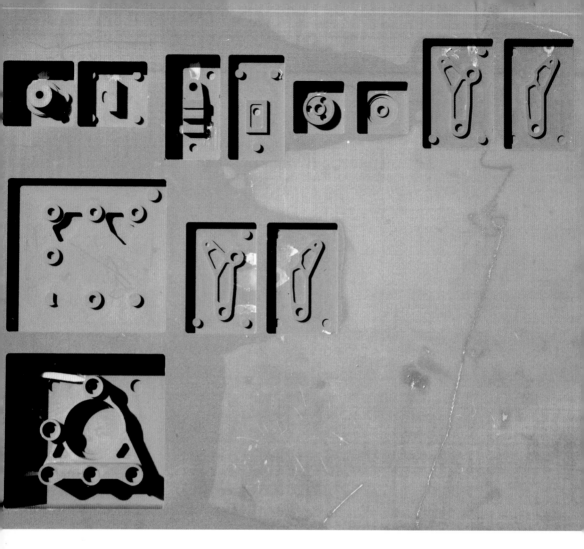

lies on a couch, head to one side
and eyes closed. To her right in
the middle of the image is a door
frame with the tell tale snake skin
hanging from it. To the right of this
is a view behind the door frame
that is clearly continuous with
Zhora's space as we see her left
elbow emerging from behind it.

We know it is hers as it has the same bangle
above the elbow, but it is displaced from her
main body. It is not a reflection as it is the correct way round. If you view sequential tracking
shot frames as stereoscopic pairs they reveal
the depth of the image. If it were a normal flat
photograph the consequence would be a flat
image. But here we find a series of flat images
at three depths. The door frame is in front, with

the two body images behind, the right hand one slightly to the rear. In practice this was probably constructed by sliding the images at different speeds in front of an animation camera to construct a sense of parallax. The effect is to construct an image between space and picture that we have to imagine into to complete. Our positional relationship is adjusted by Deckard's instructions to the computer. Through these instructions we navigate a two-dimensional image almost as if it were three dimensions. It is a similar condition to what we find when we explore Van Hoegstratten's peepshow.

In addition to the diorama camera I have built a series of picture plane studies. One, made with my colleagues Florian Koehl and Mette Thomsen, has an adjustable folding picture plane that can be inhabited. Ten cameras survey the picture plane and are synchronized to expose simultaneously. Each has a flash that can be turned off. For most of the series of ten photographs only two or three flashes are firing. The camera that fires the flash has a normal view of its shadow (no view at all as the object obscures almost all of the shadow except for that allowed by the parallax between the flash and the lens). The other cameras register the anamorphic shadows cast on the folded surface by the flashes. The cameras are arrayed round the action, some in close assemblies so that small differences can be detected while others are widely separated.

My folding picture plane drawing instrument is related to the body projects (referred to in the previous chapter), registering the experience of places at night when using the internal architecture. The figure on the picture plane is constant, although elements can be made to change colour or be bright, dim or off. It is your positional relationship to the plane that changes the image most. The folds are adjusted by registrations of your experiences as you move through the city at night. The consequential drawings are made from a sequence of photographs of the picture plane from positions matching those of the critical observer. These are then assembled on a folded picture plane that relates to the site where the journey took place.

A further series of studies involves making photographs of my studio through a replica of Van Hoegstratten's peep show where the doors are cut out. The photographs are made using a pinhole camera with a lot of sideways shift so that although the film plane is parallel to the end wall of the box, the view takes in as much of the box as possible from one of the peepholes. The camera uses a Polaroid back. The box is illuminated so that light coming through one of the doors lands on the ceiling of the box, a surface that at that point pictorially represents a continuation of the wall below it, so the light appears to land on the very wall through which it enters the room. This is only possible due the nature of the relationship between box and painting. As we tend to believe real light we believe the space even though something seems strange. These studies are in preparation for a drawing that combines many of the possibilities outlined in this chapter, a navigable drawing that implicates the

88

Acknowledgement

The work outlined in this paper would not have been possible without the help and advice of Michael Anderson of the Yale Peabody Museum. He has provided complete transparency into his own research and insights into Wilson's work, as well as providing a stimulating and critical conversation on the matter that has been exceptionally helpful.

Fragments of this section were published in the Journal of Architecture, Volume 8: Number 2 Summer 2003 page 211.
See http://www.tandf.co.uk/journals/titles/

[1]   Anthropoétrie de l'Époque Bleue (1960), Directed by Alain Jaubert, Réunion des Musées nationaux, 1997.
[2]   Habitat Dioramas. Illusions of Wilderness in Museums of Natural History. Karen Wonders
Acta Universitatis Upsaliensis, Figura Nova series 25. ISBN 91-554-3157-7, 1993
[3]   Ibid
[4]   Visual Stories, Anne Reynolds, Visual Display, Culture Beyond Appearences edited by Lynne Cook and Peter Wollen, Bay Press, ISBN0-941920-32-1, 1995
[5]   Widely published, but plate 47 in Robert Doisneau, Photofile, Thames and Hudson 1991
[6]   The Artist and the Museum Group, F.L.Jaques, Museum News 15th April 1931
[7]   Letters to Thanos Johnson, a young painter to whom Wilson provided advice and encouragement by letter over a number of years. From the archive of Michael Anderson.
[8]   Deduced from notes made by Ruth Morrill when working with Wilson.
[9]   A dual Grid system for Diorama Layout by Ruth Morrill , Curator 39/4, December 1996 Page 280-287

[10]   Explained in an unpublished interview with Wilson by Rudy Freund and Rudy Zallinger at the Peabody Museum in 1958, American Museum of Natural History Archives.

[11]   As note [2]
[12]   Raising the Standards in Natural History Dioramas: The Background Paintings of James Perry Wilson. Michael Anderson. Curator 43/4 October 2000.
[13]   The World of 3D. A practical guide to stereo photography. J.G. Ferwerda 1990
3D Book Productions. ISBN 90-71377-51-2
[14]   As note 4
[15]   L'Année dernière à Marienbad, Alain Resnais, 1961. In one famous scene an overcast sky leaves no shadows of the topiary in the garden, while the strong (painted) shadows from the actors set up an uncanny atmosphere.
[16]   Jan 3 1945, Letter to Thanos Johnson.
[17]   James Perry Wilson. Painting the Shoreline Diorama. An unpublished guide for the Yale Peabody Museum by Michael Anderson.
[18]   Later confirmed by a note on one of his moon slides at the collection of the Yale Peabody Museum of Natural History.
[19]   Perception, I Rock, New York, Scientific American Library, 1984
[20]   Blade Runner, R. Scott, Los Angeles, Warner Bros. 1982.